HIKING KENTUCKY
Scenic Trails of the Bluegrass State

About the Authors:
      *Darcy and Robert Folzenlogen are physicians and
naturalists. They have written and published a variety of
regional and national guides, including those listed above.
All of their books are dedicated to the themes of open space
protection, historic preservation and wildlife conservation.*

Cover photos (clockwise from top):
      *1. Looking south from Chained Rock, Pine Mountain
         State Resort Park*
      2. A ridgetop trail, Jefferson County Memorial Forest
      *3. Dale Hollow Lake from Eagle Point, Dale Hollow Lake
         State Park*
      *4. The Cumberland River near Eagle Falls, Cumberland
         Falls State Resort Park*

HIKING KENTUCKY
Scenic Trails of the Bluegrass State

by Darcy & Robert Folzenlogen

WILLOW PRESS
Littleton, Colorado

ISBN: 0-9620685-6-X
Library of Congress Catalog Card Number: 94-61896

Publisher: **Willow Press**
            6053 S. Platte Canyon Rd.
            Littleton, Colorado 80123

Printed by: Otto Zimmerman & Son Co., Inc.
            Newport, Kentucky

Photos by Authors
Maps by Authors, adapted from those provided by Kentucky
      State Parks, Kentucky State Nature Preserves, Ken-
      tucky Wildlife Management Areas, Daniel Boone Na-
      tional Forest and other areas covered by this guide.

For Sarah, Zach & Ally

ACKNOWLEDGEMENTS

Our sincere thanks to the many forest rangers, recreation supervisors, secretaries, park managers and other personnel who assisted us with the research and production of this guide. Special thanks to the following organizations and individuals for their contributions:

Joyce Bender, Stewardship Coordinator, Kentucky State Nature
Preserves Commission
District Rangers, Daniel Boone National Forest
Blaine A. Guthrie, Jr., Historic Middletown Inc.
Kentucky Department of Fish & Wildlife Resources
Kentucky Department of Natural Resources & Environmental
Protection
Kentucky Department of Travel Development
Kentucky State Nature Preserves Commission
Kentucky State Parks
Michael Lorton, Naturalist & Ranger, Raven Run Nature
Sanctuary
Doug Marshall, Manager, John A. Kleber Wildlife Mgmt. Area
Darrell Pennington, Recreation Technician, Redbird Purchase
Unit, Daniel Boone National Forest
Gayle Pille, Kenton County Conservation Board & Kentucky
Trail Advisory Committee
Buford Pitts, Park Manager, Freeman Lake Park
Bill Thomas, Fort Thomas Tree Commission
U.S. Army Corps of Engineers
U.S. Geological Survey, U.S. Department of the Interior
Ron Vanover, Director of Recreation & Naturalist Programs,
Jenny Wiley State Resort Park

Our thanks also to Jan Jolley at Otto Zimmerman & Son Co., Inc., for her advice and production assistance. And finally, our love and thanks to Sarah, Zach and Ally for their patience, companionship and understanding.

Darcy & Robert Folzenlogen

CONTENTS

INTRODUCTION

Stretching from the Appalachian Plateau to the Mississippi floodplain, the Commonwealth of Kentucky harbors a vast array of natural beauty. Rugged gorges, rich hardwood forests, limestone caverns, rhododendron thickets and cypress-lined waterways entice naturalists from across the globe.

Designed primarily for families and weekend explorers, this guide offers over 180 dayhikes at 62 areas across the Bluegrass State, chosen to reflect the geologic, faunal and floral diversity of Kentucky. Each hiking area is illustrated with a map and photo and a narrative describes the natural and historic features of the area. Trail mileage, local terrain and walking time are provided for each hike and travellers will appreciate the clear directions from regional cities and highways.

The hiking areas in this guide are grouped within five geographic regions of the State and an overview map is provided for each region. Chapter I introduces readers to the geomorphology of Kentucky and Chapter II covers the long, multi-day trails and wilderness areas that can be found in the State. Chapter IX presents Special Hiking Areas which are open to the public by special arrangement only.

Appendix I summarizes the Natural History of Kentucky and Appendix II lists regional conservation organizations that are working to protect that heritage. Your active and financial support for the groups in Appendix II will help to ensure the future welfare of Kentucky's wild sanctuaries.

WHEN TO GO

Hiking is an excellent form of exercise throughout the year. Though Kentucky lies well within the Temperate Zone of North America, prolonged cold and heavy snow are uncommon, even in the middle of winter. Assuming proper clothing and adequate foot gear, Kentucky's trails are accessible in all seasons.

Indeed, each season holds special rewards for outdoor adventurers. Autumn colors paint the forest in October while a mix of wildflowers carpet its floor in April. Birdwatchers flock to the swamps and marshlands each spring and fall to witness the seasonal tide of migrant waterfowl. Summer brings a colorful display to Kentucky's grasslands and the peaceful winter forest is a sure cure for cabin fever.

While novice hikers often confine their outdoor jaunts to the warmer months of the year, seasoned trekkers know that the months of October through April offer the best hiking: pesky insects are gone, summer crowds have vanished, vistas are broader and footing is often better.

Those hoping to observe resident wildlife should plan their excursion for the early morning or late daylight hours; mammals and birds tend to be most active, and thus most visible, during those times.

WHAT TO BRING

The most important requirement for any outdoor excursion is a hiking companion. Though many of us enjoy a solitary stroll through the forest, an unexpected injury can be fatal, especially in winter. Always plan your trip with someone old enough to go for help should an accident occur.

Adequate food and water should be carried on the longer hikes; these physical necessities will serve to combat dehydration, muscle cramps, hypothermia and fatigue. Sturdy, waterproof hiking boots are vital for serious trekkers and layered clothing will permit adjustment to changes in the weather.

Binoculars will add to your enjoyment of wildlife and vistas; field guides, illustrating the flora and fauna of Kentucky, are important resources for the naturalist. Insect repellent is a must during the late spring and summer, especially when visiting the State's wetlands.

LOW IMPACT HIKING

When visiting Kentucky's nature preserves, always remain on designated trails; this will minimize impact on the local ecology. Native flora should be left undisturbed and resident wildlife should be viewed from a safe and nonthreatening distance. Plan to leave your dog at home; dogs often harass wildlife and can be a nuisance to other hikers.

Pack out any trash that you bring into the preserves and pick up any that you might encounter along the way. Private property should be respected at all times and State hunting regulations must be observed to ensure everyone's safety.

Your attention to the protection of our natural resources will help to guarentee their future welfare. This can be achieved by adhering to the above recommendations and by supporting the conservation organizations listed in Appendix II.

Darcy & Robert Folzenlogen

KEY TO MAPS

Roads:

Parking Areas:

Trails:

Bridges/Boardwalks:

Stairs:

Railroads:

Lakes/Streams:

Marsh/Bog:

Forest/Woodlands:

Rock Wall/Cliffs:

3

I. THE KENTUCKY LANDSCAPE

The territory of Kentucky penetrates three of the major Geologic Provinces of North America: the Appalachian Plateau. the Interior Low Plateaus and the Gulf Coastal Plain.

THE APPALACHIAN PLATEAU

The Appalachian Plateau is a broad uplift of horizontal sediments, stretching from the Catskills of New York to northern Alabama. This Province covers western Pennsylvania, eastern Ohio, most of West Virginia, eastern Kentucky and central Tennessee.

In Kentucky, the **Pottsville Escarpment**, composed of resistant, Pennsylvanian sandstone, marks the western edge of the Appalachian Plateau, rising above the lower terrain of the Interior Low Plateaus. This edge is especially evident near Berea, Kentucky, where a chain of "knobs" stretches northeast to southwest, just a few miles east of the city. Indeed, I-75 climbs on to the Plateau just south of Berea. At the Kentucky-Virginia border, the high ridges of Pine Mountain and Cumberland Mountain represent a transition zone to the Ridge and Valley Province of North America. It is in this region of the State that the highest elevations are found, including Black Mountain (4139 feet), the pinnacle of Kentucky.

Exposed rock of the Appalachian Plateau in Kentucky is composed primarily of Carboniferous sediments, deposited in shallow seas, lakes and stream beds of the Mississippian and Pennsylvanian Periods. During that time, approximately 300 million years ago, a semi-tropical climate characterized the region and vast swamp forests covered the landscape. These primordial marshlands, home to giant amphibians and ancestral reptiles, would later decompose into the rich coal seams of eastern Kentucky.

Today, the uplifted Plateau is covered by an extensive forest of hardwood and pine and has been carved into a maze of valleys and ridges by a vast network of streams. The Big Sandy, Licking, Kentucky and Cumberland Rivers drain Kentucky's portion of the Appalachian Plateau. Wild turkeys, pileated woodpeckers, white-tailed deer and an increasing number of black bear inhabit this rugged landscape which, in many areas, has succumbed to farms, logging and strip mines.

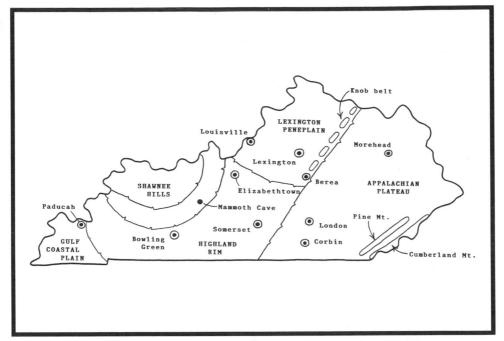

THE GEOLOGICAL PROVINCES OF KENTUCKY

THE INTERIOR LOW PLATEAUS

In Kentucky, the Interior Low Plateaus is subdivided into three regions: the Lexington Peneplain, the Shawnee Hills and the Highland Rim.

The **Lexington Peneplain**, also called the Bluegrass Region, is a rolling landscape centered above the Jessamine Dome, an upwelling of deep Precambrain rock along the "Cincinnati Arch." Exposed rock throughout the central regions of the Peneplain are middle Ordovician limestones which have eroded to yield the rich soil of Kentucky's horse country; these are the oldest exposed rock in the State. The outer sections of the **Lexington Peneplain**, forming a broad, semicircular swath, from Louisville to Richmond to Maysville, is underlaid with Silurian and Devonian rock (limestones and shales).

To the north, the **Lexington Peneplain** is bounded by the Ohio River and, to the east, by the Appalachian Plateau. Along its western and southern border is the **Muldraugh's Hill Escarpment**, the northern edge of the Highland Rim, which rises up to 600 feet above the outer Peneplain. This escarpment, composed of early Mississippian sandstones, stretches across I-65 a few miles north of Elizabethtown.

Bisected by the Green River, the **Shawnee Hills Province** is bordered by the **Dripping Springs Escarpment**, a low, irregular uplift which runs from Elizabethtown southward along the west side of I-65 to Bowling Green and thence northwestward to the Ohio River. The Escarpment itself is composed

5

of late Mississippian sandstone which overlies a thick layer of Mississippian limestone, creating ideal conditions for limestone cave formation; indeed, **Mammoth Cave** is located within the outer belt of the **Shawnee Hills**. Inner portions of this region, rimmed by the **Pottsville Escarpment** (comparable to the western edge of the Appalachian Plateau), sit atop Pennsylvanian rock (sandstone and coal).   The **Shawnee Hills Province** extends northward into southern Indiana.

South-central Kentucky is known geologically as the **Highland Rim**, a gently rolling landscape that is now characterized by some of the State's largest reservoirs: Green River Lake, Lake Cumberland, Dale Hollow Lake and Barren River Lake.   That portion of the Highland Rim south and southwest of Bowling Green is often called the **Pennyroyal Plain**, a karst plain of few surface streams, dotted with numerous sinkholes.   Exposed rock throughout the Highland Rim is Mississippian in age, except for a small area of Cretaceous deposits within the southernmost section of Kentucky's Land Between the Lakes.

THE GULF COASTAL PLAIN

West of Kentucky Lake (the lower Tennessee River), the **Gulf Coastal Plain** begins: a low, flat landscape of marshlands, floodplain forest and baldcypress swamps. Having been covered by a northern arm of the Gulf of Mexico through much of the Mesozoic and Cenozoic Eras, westernmost Kentucky is now characterized by sandy soil and few rock formations. Poorly compacted Tertiary sandstones and loose Quaternary gravels underlie the thin soil. Clearly, this is the "youngest" part of the State.

Baldcypress swamp on the Gulf Coastal Plain

II. KENTUCKY'S LONG TRAILS & WILDERNESS AREAS

While this Guide is devoted to illustrating and describing dayhikes throughout the Commonwealth of Kentucky, we would be remiss not to provide an overview of the State's long, backpacking trails and Wilderness Areas. Portions of these multi-day routes will be encountered at many of the Hiking Areas covered in the book.

North-South Trail. This 60-mile path stretches the length of the Land Between the Lakes National Recreation Area in western Kentucky and western Tennessee. The northernmost 40 miles lie within Kentucky and can be accessed from a number of locations within the Recreation Area. Back-country camping is allowed within Land Between the Lakes but permits must be obtained at the Welcome Stations or Visitor Center. See Hiking Area #4 for more details.

Mammoth Cave National Park. A vast network of back-country trails, which connect a number of primitive campgrounds, are located within the Park, north of the Green River. Those planning overnight excursions must register at the Visitor Center or Ranger Station. Refer to Hiking Area #15 for an overview of this area.

Beaver Creek Wilderness Area. This rugged, undeveloped wilderness encompasses 4800 acres along the Beaver Creek drainage in McCreary County. The preserve lies within Daniel Boone National Forest and is part of the Beaver Creek Wildlife Management Area. Old logging roads provide access to this remote landscape of sandstone cliffs, "rock houses," scenic waterfalls and rich woodlands. Back-country camping is permitted. For more information, contact the Somerset District Ranger, U.S. Forest Service, 156 Realty Lane, Somerset, KY 42501; 606-679-2018.

Sheltowee Trace Trail. "Sheltowee," meaning "Big Turtle," was the name given to Daniel Boone by the native Indians. It is thus fitting that the State's longest trail, Forest Trail #100, has been designated the Sheltowee Trace Trail. This 257-mile path runs the entire length of Daniel Boone National Forest, from Pickett State Park, in Tennessee, to Rowan County, Kentucky, north of Morehead. The Trail is easily accessed at a number of Parks and Recreation Areas throughout the National Forest, including the Big South Fork National Recreation Area, Cumberland Falls State Resort Park, Laurel River Lake, Natural Bridge State Resort Park, Red River Gorge National Recreation Area and Cave Run Lake. The map on page 8 provides an overview of the Trail's route; numbers on the map correspond to Hiking Areas in this guide from which the Sheltowee Trace can be accessed.

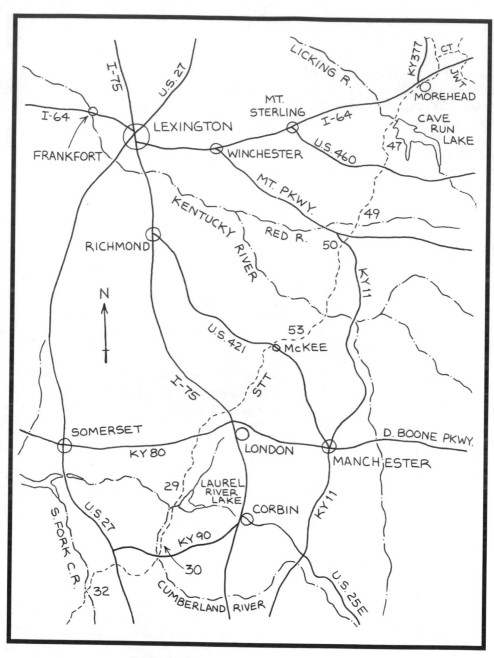

THE SHELTOWEE TRACE TRAIL

The Sheltowee Trace Trail near Turkeyfoot Recreation Area

The Kentucky Trail. This 27-mile trail winds along the west wall of the Big South Fork Valley, from the Peters Mountain Trailhead to the Yamacraw Bridge. The entire route, which undulates across numerous drainages, lies within the Big South Fork National Recreation Area and is illustrated in Hiking Area #32.

Red River Gorge National Recreation Area. Characterized by over 80 natural arches and spectacular sandstone cliffs, this 25,662-acre wonderland is accessed by over 36 miles of hiking trails. The **Long Hunters Trek**, a popular back-packing route, covers 13.1 miles; this loop hike begins and ends at the Koomer Ridge Campground, off Ky 15. The route uses Trails 220, 221, 223 and 226 in sequence (see map in Hiking Area #49). Back-country camping is permitted within the Recreation Area. For directions to this magnificent preserve and for a discussion of dayhikes within Red River Gorge, please refer to Hiking Area #49.

Clifty Wilderness Area. This 13,300 acre refuge adjoins the Red River Gorge National Recreation Area, protecting areas east and north of KY 715. Like the Recreation Area, it harbors many scenic rock formations and is home to over 15 endangered plant species. Back-country camping is permitted in the Wilderness; for information, call 606-663-2852.

Redbird Crest Trail. Named for "Redbird," a Cherokee Chief, this 65-mile loop trail follow ridgetops above the Redbird River Valley in Clay and Leslie Counties. Access is best achieved at the Forest Ranger Station on KY 66 south of the Daniel Boone Parkway. For directions and more information, see Hiking Area #58.

The Ridge Trail. Located within **Cumberland Gap National Historic Park**, this 16.6-mile trail (33.2 miles roundtrip), follows the crest of Cumberland Mountain, from the Pinnacle Overlook to the White Rocks (Virginia). The trail stays close to the Kentucky-Virginia line and several connecting trails ascend from both sides of the ridge. Please refer to Hiking Area #62 for a map and more details.

The Little Shepherd Trail. Following the crest of Pine Mountain, this gravel road (paved near its western end) is 38 miles in length. Its eastern terminus is at the entrance to Pine Mountain Wildlife Management Area, on U.S. 119, south of Whitesburg. The Trail crosses through Kingdom Come State Park (see Hiking Area #60) along the way and six miles of the route, near its western terminus, wind through Kentenia State Forest. The western trailhead is off the east side of U.S. 421, north of Harlan.

THE LITTLE SHEPHERD TRAIL

The Jenny Wiley-Michael Tygart-Simon Kenton Trail System. Named for Jenny Wiley, a pioneer heroine who was captured by and later escaped from the Shawnee Indians, the **Jenny Wiley Trail** covers 163 miles and winds through nine Kentucky Counties. The route utilizes a series of woodland paths and country roads, leading from Jenny Wiley State Resort Park (JWSRP), near Prestonsburg, to South Portsmouth, on the Ohio River. Much of the route crosses private property and backpackers should respect the privacy and rights of the land owners.

Designated a National Heritage Trail by the U.S. Department of the Interior, the **Jenny Wiley Trail** was established to create an avenue for day-hikes and backpacking trips in eastern Kentucky. Historic landmarks and primitive campgrounds are spaced along the Trail and access can be achieved from Jenny Wiley State Park or from a number of towns along the route (see map on page 11).

The **Jenny Wiley Trail** can also be accessed via three connecting trails. The **Michael Tygart Trail (MTT)**, a 24-mile backpacking trail, originates at Greenbo Lake State Resort Park (see Hiking Area #44) while the 9-mile **Simon Kenton Trail (SKT)** begins at Carter Caves State Resort Park (CCSRP; see Hiking Area #43); both lead westward to intersect the **Jenny Wiley Trail**. A third **Connector Trail (CT)** leads eastward from the **Sheltowee Trace Trail (STT)**, northeast of Morehead, off KY 377 (see map).

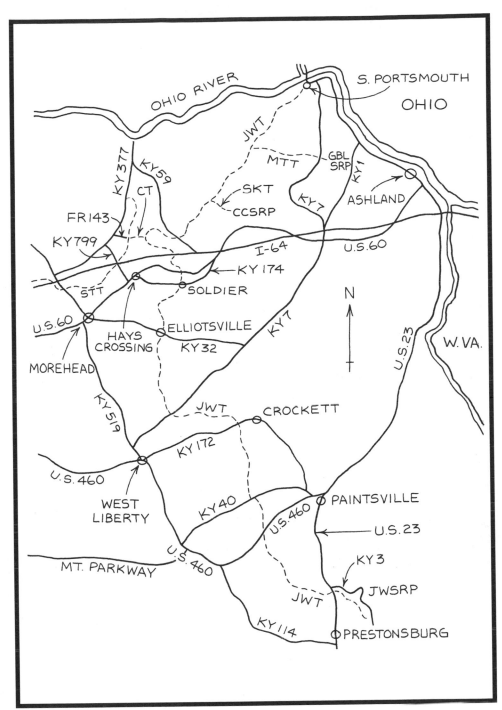

THE JENNY WILEY-MICHAEL TYGART-SIMON KENTON TRAIL SYSTEM

III. KENTUCKY HIKING AREAS

1. Ballard Wildlife Mgmt. Area
2. Columbus-Belmont State Park
3. Reelfoot National Wildlife Refuge
4. Land Between the Lakes N.R.A.
5. Lake Barkley State Resort Park
6. Pennyrile Forest State Res. Park
7. Higginson-Henry W.M.A.
8. Sauerheber Wildlife Mgmt. Area
9. John James Audubon State Park
10. Yellowbank W.M.A.
11. Otter Creek Park
12. Jefferson Memorial Forest
13. Rough River Dam State Resort Park
14. Freeman Lake
15. Mammoth Cave Nat. Park
16. Lake Malone State Park
17. Logan Co. Glade Nat. Preserve
18. Cherokee Park
19. Beargrass Creek State N.P.
20. Taylorsville Lake State Park
21. Bernheim Research Forest
22. Buckley Hills Nature Preserve
23. Raven Run Nature Sanctuary
24. Abraham Lincoln Birthplace National Historic Site
25. Green River Lake State Park
26. Barren River Lake S.R.P.
27. Lake Cumberland S.R.P.
28. Dale Hollow State Park
29. Laurel Lake & Vicinity
30. Cumberland Falls S.R.P.
31. Natural Arch Scenic Area

32. Big South Fork N.R.A.
33. Boone County Cliffs State Nature Preserve
34. Highland Cemetery Forest
35. Ft. Thomas Landmark Tree Trail
36. Doe Run Lake
37. Big Bone Lick State Park
38. Kincaid Lake State Park
39. Mullins Wildlife Mgmt. Area
40. Quiet Trails State N.P.
41. Kleber Wildlife Mgmt. Area
42. Blue Licks Battlefield State Park
43. Carter Caves State Resort Park
44. Greenbo Lake State Resort Park
45. Jesse Stuart State Nature Preserve
46. Grayson Lake
47. Cave Run Lake & Vicinity
48. Spencer-Morton Preserve
49. Red River Gorge N.R.A.
50. Natural Bridge State Resort Park
51. Central Kentucky W.M.A.
52. Berea College Forest
53. Turkey Foot Recreation Area
54. Buckhorn Lake State Resort Park
55. Paintsville Lake
56. Jenny Wiley State Resort Park
57. Levi Jackson State Park
58. Redbird Crest Trail
59. Bad Branch State Nature Preserve
60. Kingdom Come State Park
61. Pine Mountain State Resort Park
62. Cumberland Gap National Historic Park

B - Beaver Creek Wilderness Area

C - Clifty Wilderness Area

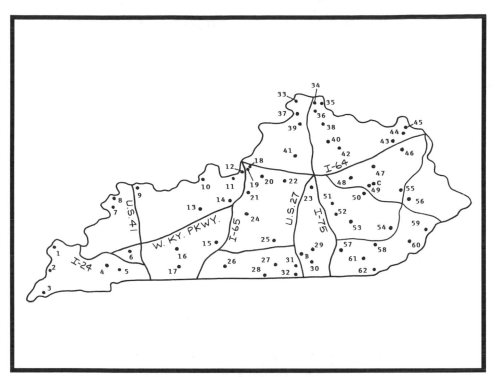

KENTUCKY HIKING AREAS

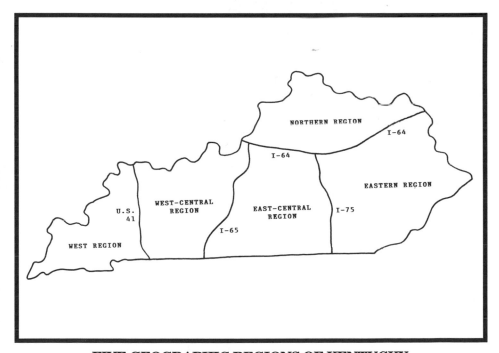

FIVE GEOGRAPHIC REGIONS OF KENTUCKY

IV. HIKING AREAS OF WESTERN KENTUCKY

1. Ballard Wildlife Management Area

2. Columbus-Belmont State Park

3. Reelfoot National Wildlife Refuge

4. Land Between the Lakes
   National Recreation Area

5. Lake Barkley State Resort Park

6. Pennyrile Forest State Resort Park

7. Higginson-Henry Wildlife
   Management Area

8. Sauerheber Wildlife Management Area

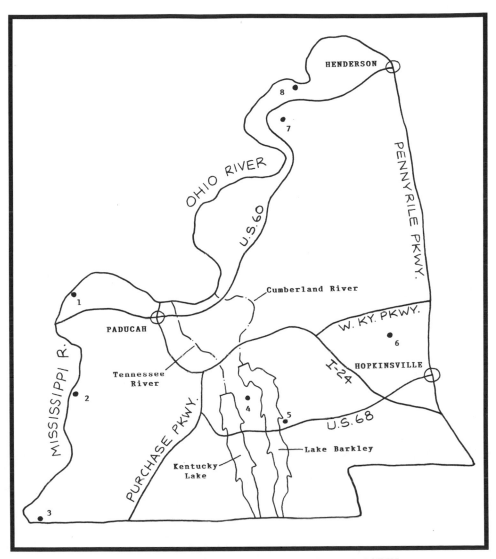

HIKING AREAS OF WESTERN KENTUCKY

1 BALLARD WILDLIFE MANAGEMENT AREA

Loop 1
   Distance: 6.4 miles
   Terrain: flat
   Walking Time: 4 hours

Loop 2
   Distance: 5.2 miles
   Terrain: flat
   Walking time: 3 hours

Loop 3
   Distance: 7.4 miles
   Terrain: flat
   Walking time: 5 hours

A chain of wildlife management areas stretch along the floodplains of the Ohio and Mississippi Rivers in western Kentucky. Established to provide migratory reststops and wintering grounds for waterfowl, these open lands are characterized by baldcypress swamps, riparian woodlands, crop fields and seasonal wetlands. To protect the wintering waterfowl, the refuges are closed to the public from October 15 through March 15. Nevertheless, they offer superb settings for hiking and nature study for much of the year.

Ballard Wildlife Management Area, 8 miles north of Barlow, is one of the more interesting and accessible preserves in the region. This 8373-acre refuge is home to bald eagles, river otters, wild turkeys and white-tailed deer. Red-headed woodpeckers and belted kingfishers patrol the baldcypress swamps while killdeer, bobwhite quail and an excellent variety of raptors will be found on the open croplands. Herons and egrets are abundant during the warmer months and the refuge was the site of Kentucky's first bald eagle nest in more than 40 years (1986).

Directions: From I-24 near Paducah, take Exit 4 and head west on U.S. 60; drive 21 miles to Barlow and turn north on Ky 1105. Proceed 8.2 miles and bear left on Ky 473. Continue another 2.3 miles and turn left into the refuge.

Routes: While there are no foot-trails at Ballard WMA, a network of gravel roads provide access to the preserve and yield a variety of potential day hikes. We suggest the following routes.

Loop 1 (6.4 miles). Park at the campgrounds along the shore of **Shelby Lake (SL)** and hike northwestward to the **Oscar Bottoms (OB)**. Turn left at the intersection, heading southwest through this floodplain habitat. Bypass the cutoff to **Little Turner Lake (LTL)**, soon hiking past **Goose Pond (GP)**. Turn left at the next intersection and, after crossing a bridge, head northeast along the shores of **Butler (BL)** and **Big Turner Lakes (BTL)**. Pass the **Middle Landing Campground (MLCG)**, bear left at the next two intersections and proceed back to the **Shelby Lake Campgrounds** (see map).

Loop 2 (5.2 miles). This hike begins and ends at the **Headquarters Building (HQ)**, making an elongated loop to the south and circling **Mitchell Lake (ML)**. An extensive planting of sunflowers stretches along the west shore and this lake is one of the better sites to find bald eagles at the refuge.

16

*Baldcypress swamp
at Ballard W.M.A.*

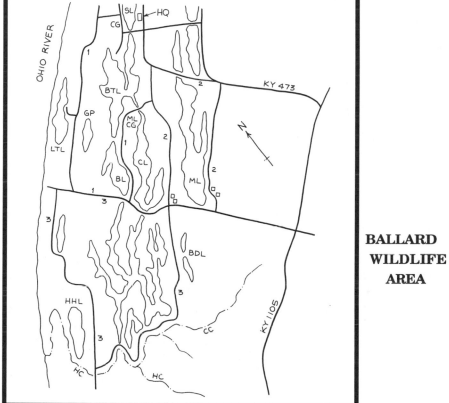

**BALLARD
WILDLIFE
AREA**

Loop 3 (7.4 miles). Park at the intersection just SW of **Mitchell Lake (ML)** and hike to the SSW, passing the **Beaver Dam Lakes (BDL)**. The road turns westward along **Clanton Creek (CC)** and then angles NW above **Humphrey Creek (HC)**, crossing through a rich riparian woodland. Turn right at the intersection, passing **Happy Hollow Lake (HHL)**, and continue northward to the **Oscar Bottoms**. Return to your car along the road which leads to the southeast, crossing the shallows of **Butler (BL)** and **Caster Lakes (CL)**.

17

2 COLUMBUS-BELMONT STATE PARK

Distance: 1.8 miles
Terrain: rolling
Walking time: 1.5 hours

Commanding a spectacular view of the Mississippi River, **Columbus-Belmont State Park** occupies the former site of Fort De Russey, a Confederate military outpost during the Civil War. This well-fortified encampment, protected by floating gunboats and cliff-top cannons, was under the command of General Leonidas Polk.

The "Battle of Belmont" was engaged in November, 1861, when General Ulysses S. Grant opened the Union's Western Campaign. Grant destroyed Belmont, on the Missouri shore, but was overpowered at "the Gibraltar of the West" and retreated upriver. The Union troops returned in early 1862, cutting off supply lines to Columbus and forcing the Confederate army to evacuate the site.

A 1.8 mile walk, described below, takes you through this 156-acre Park which harbors a fascinating collection of artifacts from the War Between the States.

Directions: The Park is on the western edge of Columbus. From I-24, take U.S. 62 west to Bardwell and then Ky 123 south to Columbus. From the Purchase Parkway, take Ky 80 west to Columbus. Once in the town, watch for signs to the State Park. The Park is open April through October.

Route: From the parking lot, hike northward and enter the Confederate trenches, making a figure 8 through this historic fortress and climbing on to **Arrowhead Point (AP)** along the way. Exiting near a **picnic shelter (P)**, you are treated to a spectacular view of the grand Mississippi. After taking in the sights, follow the paved walkway that leads southward above the cliffs, passing the **Chain & Anchor Memorial (C/A)** and continuing out to another **Lookout Shelter (LS)**. Plan to stop by the **Park Museum (M)** which houses Civil War and Native American artifacts; the small admission fee also covers a slide program on the Battle of Belmont. The Museum is open daily, May through September; weekends only in April and October.

Continue along the paved walkway and then angle to the south on a foot path that leads out to the bluffs and cuts through a second set of trenches (see map). Exiting near the **Campgrounds**, turn right and follow the road to a **Cemetery (C)** which contains many graves from the Civil War era. Circle through the Cemetery, turn right on the roadway and return to your car via a wide pathway that cuts behind the maintenance and office buildings (see map).

The Park commands spectacular views of the Mississippi

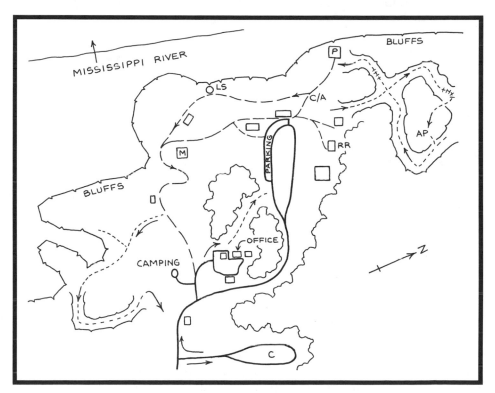

COLUMBUS-BELMONT STATE PARK

19

3 REELFOOT NATIONAL WILDLIFE REFUGE

Distance: 7.0 miles
Terrain: flat
Walking time: 4.5 hours

Many of us who inhabit the interior of North America feel immune to the natural catastrophes that continue to mold our Continent. While hurricanes lash the southeast, earthquakes rearrange California and Cascade volcanos threaten the Pacific Northwest, we fear only the occasional tornados that streak across the landscape. But if the Great Flood of 1993 did not shake your security, perhaps the story of **Reelfoot Lake** will convince you that the entire planet is subject to periodic upheavels.

During the winter of 1811-1812 a series of powerful earthquakes shook the mid Mississippi Valley, altering the course of the River and creating a mammoth depression east of the channel. River waters spilled into this newly-established lowland, giving birth to the 20,000 acre lake. One hundred and thirty years later, **Reelfoot National Wildlife Refuge** was established to protect this beautiful lake and its surrounding wetlands. The refuge teems with life throughout the year but is especially important as wintering habitat for waterfowl and bald eagles. Ospreys, egrets and Mississippi kites are among the summer residents.

While most of the refuge (and all of Reelfoot Lake) lies within the borders of Tennessee, a small portion juts into Kentucky. We offer a 7 mile walk which leads through this northernmost section of the preserve.

Directions: From Hickman, in extreme southwest Kentucky, follow Ky 94 toward the southwest. Drive almost 10 miles and turn left on a gravel road just beyond a railroad crossing; this turnoff is 2.8 miles past the town of Sassafras Ridge. A National Wildlife Refuge sign is posted at this junction but, at the time of our visit, faced south and was easy to miss.

Turn left on the gravel road and proceed 1 mile to the Refuge entrance, on your right. Leave your car near refuge building (see map) and be sure to carry plenty of water and nourishment on this long, open country hike. The Refuge is open dawn to dusk, every day of the year.

Route: From the entry area, hike southward along the gravel road and turn left at the intersection for a 2 mile trek to a wooded lake. White-tailed deer may be spotted on the open fields and the lake offers prime habitat for wood ducks, purple gallinules and red-headed woodpeckers. Water lilies blanket the shallows during the warmer months, home to a superb variety of frogs, turtles and snakes.

Backtrack along the gravel road and continue westward at the intersection, crossing through open woodlands, swamp forest and wet meadows. Warblers are abundant here in April and northern harriers patrol the grasslands throughout the year. Resident mammals, including red fox, o-

20

Water lilies blanket a pond at the Reelfoot Refuge

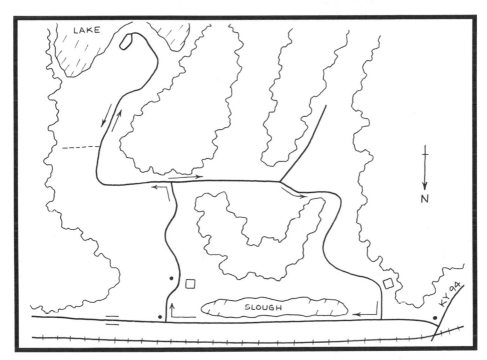

REELFOOT N.W.R. (KENTUCKY SECTION)

possums, raccoons, mink and swamp rabbits are best found at dawn or dusk. After passing an old barn you will intersect the roadway that leads to the Refuge entrance from Ky 94 (see map). Turn right, hiking along a shallow slough, and return to your car.

4 LAND BETWEEN THE LAKES

North-South Trail
  Distance: up to 40 miles in Ky
  Terrain: rolling; hilly areas
  Walking time: up to 30 hours in Ky

Canal Loop Trails
  Distance: 1-7 miles
  Terrain: rolling
  Walking time: 1-4.5 hrs.

Woodlands Nature Center Trails
  Distance: .2 to 5 miles
  Terrain: rolling
  Walking time: .5-3 hours

Wranglers Trails
  Distance: 2.9-12.1 miles
  Terrain: hilly
  Walking time: 2-8 hours

Land Between the Lakes is a 270 square-mile National Recreation Area in western Kentucky and western Tennessee. The northern 2/3 of this 40 mile peninsula, which is flanked by Kentucky Lake to the west and Lake Barkley to the east, lies within the State of Kentucky.

The history of this 170,000 acre refuge dates back to 1944 when the Tennessee Valley Authority constructed a dam on the lower Tennessee River, creating Kentucky Lake. When work began on the Lake Barkley Dam on the Cumberland River, in 1959, the TVA proposed that the "Land Between the Lakes" be set aside as a National Recreation Area. The Kennedy Administration approved the project in 1963 and further development was funded by the Public Works Appropriation Act of 1964. Lake Barkley was impounded in 1965 and the **Land Between the Lakes** has since become one of the most popular recreation sites in the country.

More than a park for fishermen, hunters and tourists, the **Land Between the Lakes** protects vast stands of second-growth, hardwood forest which is home to an excellent variety of wildlife. White-tailed deer, coyotes, red fox and a number of smaller mammals roam the peninsula and 248 species of birds have been identified here. Bald eagles have long wintered in the area and the first active bald eagle nest at **LBL** was documented in 1984.

With the establishment of the **Woodlands Nature Center (WNC)** on Honker Bay, the Recreation Area has become a vital center of environmental education. The **Nature Center** houses natural history exhibits, displays native wildlife species and conducts nature study programs across the peninsula. Among other projects, the Center takes part in the captive propagation of red wolves, a program administered by the American Association of Zoological Parks & Aquariums. In addition, **LBL** maintains a herd of American bison on a 200 acre range, just south of the Kentucky border.

Access to the back-country of **Land Between the Lakes** is provided by a 250 mile network of trails. The **North-South Trail (NST)** stretches for 60 miles, from the Barkley Canal to the South Welcome Station (in Tennessee); approximately 40 miles of this trail cross through the Kentucky portion of **LBL**. Less formidable trail networks are found at the **Woodlands Nature Center (WNC)**, at **Wranglers Campground (WC)** and at the north end of the peninsula (the **Canal Loop Trails, CLT**).

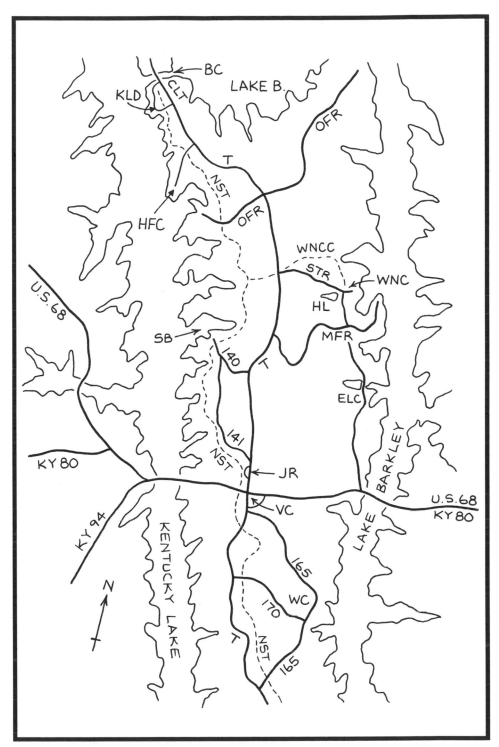

LAND BETWEEN THE LAKES N.R.A. (KY SECTION)

While the **Land Between the Lakes** is an appealing destination during any season of the year, back-country explorers should know that insects-- especially ticks--can be a nuisance during the warmer months. Use of a chemical repellent, clothing to cover arms and legs, frequent skin checks and a broad-brimmed hat are all recommended to combat ticks. We suggest that you plan your hiking excursions for late fall or winter.

Directions: From I-24, east of Paducah, take Exit #31 and head south on Ky Route 453 toward Grand Rivers. Within 4.5 miles you will cross the Barkley Canal and enter the Land Between the Lakes. For an overview of the Recreation Area, plan to stop at the Golden Pond Visitor Center (VC), located at the intersection of The Trace (T) and U.S. 68/Ky 80 (see map).

Routes: As noted above, there are 250 miles of designated trails at Land Between the Lakes. While some of these are in Tennessee, there are plenty of hiking opportunities in the Kentucky portion of the Recreation Area. We have grouped our recommendations within four areas:

NORTH-SOUTH TRAIL

North-South Trail (NST): Stretching for 60 miles, from the Barkley Canal to the South Welcome Station (in Tennessee), this trail is a bit long for most day hikers! However, backpackers may want to tackle its entire route and back-country camping is permitted at **LBL** (obtain overnight permits at either the North or the South Welcome Stations).

Approximately 40 miles of the **North-South Trail** is located north of the Kentucky-Tennessee border and plenty of access points allow day hikers to make "out-and-back" excursions on the trail. Alternatively, by using two cars, a number of long day hikes can be planned. We suggest the following routes (distances are one-way):

> **Jenny Ridge Picnic Area (JR) to Sugar Bay Access (SB; at end of Road 140) - 9 miles; 6 hours**
>
> **Hillman Ferry Campground (HFC) to Old Ferry Road (OFR) -4 miles; 3 hours**
>
> **Fords Bay Road (Road 170) south to Roads 165/172 (near Tennessee border) - 5.5 miles; 4 hours**

CANAL LOOP TRAILS

Canal Loop Trails: A network of hiking trails, in combination with the northernmost section of the **North South Trail (NST)**, form a variety of loop hikes through the northern tip of **Land Between the Lakes**. These trails are accessed from **Kentucky Lake Drive (Road 101),** from **Road 102** or from the **North Welcome Station (NWS)**.

The outermost route (circling the entire area; see map) yields a hike of approximately 7 miles (walking time: 4.5 hours). The shortest loops, each about 1 mile in length are found west of **The Trace**, at either end of the network (see map); these small loops each use a section of the **North-South Trail**. As is evident from the map, hikers can plan other routes of varying length, depending on time limitations and their level of fitness.

Kentucky Lake from Road 101

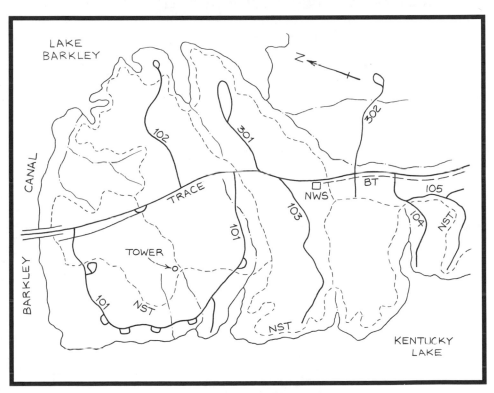

CANAL LOOP TRAILS

Woodland Nature Center Trails. A variety of trails originate at or near the Nature Center which is reached by taking the **Silver Trail Road (STR)** east from **The Trace**; the turnoff to this road is 10.5 miles south of the Barkley Canal. The parking lots and trails are open 9am-5pm, March through November, and 9am-4pm on weekends only, December through February.

Hematite Lake Trail (2.2 miles; walking time of 1.5 hrs.). This elongated loop begins at a parking lot just southwest of the **Center Furnace (CF)** and circles Hematite Lake, the former reservoir for the town of Hematite. This town arose during the iron-production era of the mid-late 1800s. Today, only the old furnace stack and scattered artifacts remain but the lake itself provides habitat for a variety of waterfowl, turtles, snakes and amphibians. Resident mammals, including deer, raccoons, opossum and mink, may be spotted near the shore at dawn or dusk.

Honker Trail (HT; 5 miles; walking time of 3 hrs.). Access to this loop trail is via paths that descend from either side of the **Nature Center (WNC)** parking lot. The trail itself circles an inlet of Honker Bay, cutting through adjacent meadows and woodlands. This is an excellent hike for birdwatchers, providing an opportunity to see waterfowl, ospreys, bald eagles and numerous songbirds.

The **Woodland Walk (WW; .7 mile)** and **Waterfowl Loop (WL; .4 mile)**, combined with access paths from either side of the Nature Center parking lot, yield a total hike of approximately 1.5 miles. These trails wind through forest and marshlands just west of Honker Bay.

The **Long Creek Trail (LCT; .2 mile)** is a self-guided, paved pathway that begins on a side road just east of the **Center Furnace (CF)** and leads down to the banks of Long Creek. A rich diversity of plantlife will be found along the trail.

The **Center Furnace Trail (CFT; .3 mile)** starts at a parking lot on Silver Trail Road and winds through the former site of **Hematite**, a 19th Century iron production center.

WRANGLERS CAMPGROUND AREA

The Wranglers Campground Trails. This network of trail loops, which range in length from 2.9 to 12 miles, is designed for horsemen but can be used by hikers as well. **Wranglers Campground** is located east of **The Trace (T)** and is best reached via **Road 165** which angles southeastward, just south of the **Golden Pond Visitor Center (VC).**

The map on the facing page illustrates the trail loops, numbered **1 through 6,** all of which originate at the Campground. Since they are heavily used by horsemen, sections of the trails, especially near stream crossings, can become quagmires during the spring and summer months. Most of this area is covered by second-growth hardwood forest but meadows and open woodlands will be found near Road 165. Trail mileages are as follows: Trail 1 - 6 miles, Trail 2 - 2.9 miles, Trail 3 - 3.5 miles, Trail 4 - 2.9 miles, Trail 5 - 7.3 miles, Trail 6 - 12.1 miles.

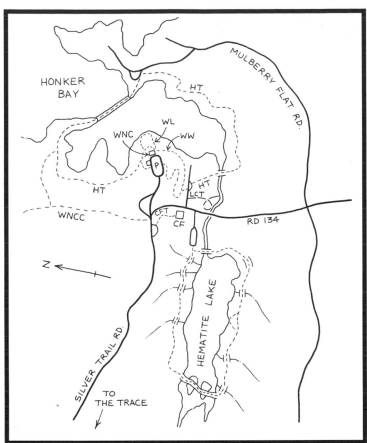

WOODLANDS NATURE CENTER TRAILS

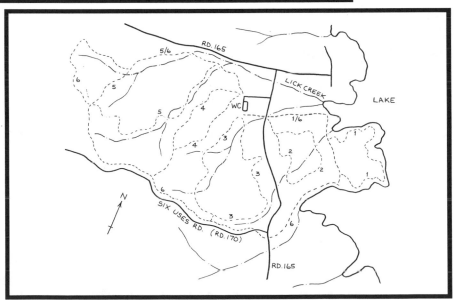

WRANGLERS CAMPGROUND TRAILS

5 LAKE BARKLEY STATE RESORT PARK

L.M. Phillips Memorial Trail
Distance: .7 mile loop
Terrain: rolling
Walking time: .75 hour

Stable Trail
Distance: 3 mi. roundtrip
Terrain: hilly
Walking time: 2 hours

Beach Trail
Distance: 4.5 miles roundtrip
Terrain: hilly
Walking time: 3 hours

Wilderness Trail
Distance: 1.8 mile loop
Terrain: rolling
Walking time: 1.5 hours

Drowned by a T.V.A. reservoir in 1965, the lower Cumberland River Valley has given rise to Lake Barkley, a paradise for boaters and fishermen. Lake Barkley State Resort Park sits above the eastern shore of this beautiful lake, providing year-round recreation for thousands of visitors.

The Park offers four hiking trails, all of which originate near the Lodge. A fifth path, the .3 mile **Wagon Wheel Trail (WWT)**, leads from the Campground to the Beach.

Directions: The entrance to the Park is on the north side of U.S. 68. From I-24, exit onto U.S.68, head west and drive almost 13 miles to the Park entrance, on your right; the entry road is 6.5 miles west of Cadiz.

Routes: Lena M. Phillips Memorial Trail (LT). This .7 mile loop begins east of the Lodge; descend a stairway from the playground to reach the trailhead. Thirteen educational plaques are spaced along this self-guided trail and brochures are available at the Recreation Office. The path crosses through a moist woodland, fording numerous drainages along the way.

Stable Trail (ST). This trail is accessed by a connector trail which cuts off from the Lena Phillips Trail (LT) between stations 4 and 5. Branching to the east, the **Stable Trail** climbs steadily to the Park Road, emerging just north of the Stables. The roundtrip hike from the Lodge to the Stables via this path is approximately 3 miles.

Beach Trail (BT). This trail also originates off the connector trail that leads away from the Lena Phillips Trail (LT) between stations 4 and 5. The **Beach Trail** is not a casual stroll along the shore; rather, the trail negotiates the edge of a ridge, climbing through cedar glades and undulating across several drainages before dropping to the lake shore. The roundtrip hike from the Lodge to the Beach is approximately 4.5 miles.

Wilderness Trail (WT). Despite its name, this is the least "wild" and most pleasant hike at the Park. The trail begins across from the Lodge access bridge where a sign indicates "Nature Trail." Cutting east from the paved walkway, the **Wilderness Trail** circles above a drainage, winds through a hardwood forest and ends at the edge of a scenic bay. Return to the Lodge via the open field and Park roadway, completing a hike of 1.8 miles.

The Wilderness Trail ends at a scenic bay

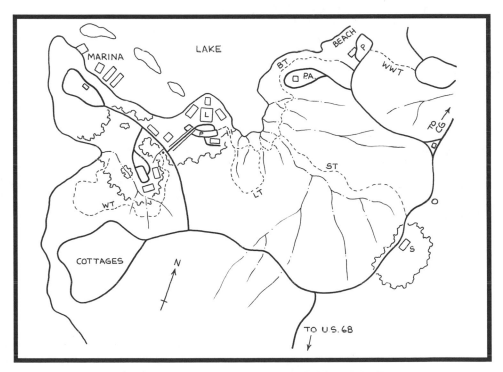

LAKE BARKLEY STATE RESORT PARK

6 PENNYRILE FOREST STATE RESORT PARK

Combined Loop Hike
  Distance: 4 miles
  Terrain: hilly
  Walking time: 2.5 hours

Lake Trail Loop
  Distance: 1.75 miles
  Terrain: hilly
  Walking time: 1.5 hrs.

Enamored with the natural beauty and abundant game of the Tradewater Valley, John Thompson, a native of Virginia, established his homestead at the present-day site of **Pennyrile Forest State Resort Park** in 1808. The U.S. Department of Agriculture acquired most of the forest in the late 1930s, conveying it to the Kentucky Division of Forestry in 1946. The State Park itself was opened in the summer of 1954 and has since become a popular destination for the residents and tourists of western Kentucky.

Surrounded by over 15,000 acres of State Forest, **Pennyrile Forest State Resort Park** offers an excellent setting for day hikes. Five trails provide access to the Park's varied habitats and we suggest two loops, both of which originate at the Lodge.

Directions: From the Western Kentucky Parkway, exit at Dawson Springs and head south on Ky 109. The Park entrance is on the west side of the road, approximately 5 miles south of Dawson Springs. Park at the Lodge.

Routes: Combined Loop Hike (4 miles). From the Lodge parking lot, hike northward on the road that leads toward the Golf Course (see map). Proceed a short distance and angle right onto the **Indian Bluffs Trail (IBT)**, which climbs past outcroppings of Mississippian sandstone. Overlying less resistent layers of shale and limestone, this sandstone has eroded into a scenic gallery of ledges, recessed caves and natural arches. The caves were used for shelter by local Indians as recently as 300 years ago.

Descend to the Park road and turn left at the intersection, crossing Clifty Creek. Pick up the **Clifty Creek Trail (CCT)** which parallels the stream and leads to the base of the Pennyrile Dam. Climb back to the Cottage access road and hike southward to its terminal loop. Angle right on the **Cane Trail (CT)** which makes a 1.25 mile excursion through the forest; the trail is named for patches of wild cane that grow along the lower woodland drainages.

Upon reaching the **Lake Trail (LT)**, turn right and cross the southern inlet of Pennyrile Lake. You will soon pass a Pump Station (P), a forest service road and a lakeside gazebo, where the **Pennyroyal Trail (PRT)** cuts away to the east. Turn on to this trail which circles of forested knob where wild mint (American Pennyroyal) used to grow in abundance. After hiking approximately .75 mile, you will reach a picnic shelter and trail intersection; turn left, walking above rocky bluffs, and then descend to the sidestream via a stairway; you are now back on the **Lake Trail**. Ascend past the beach area, cross another stream and return to the Lodge.

A view from the Lake Trail

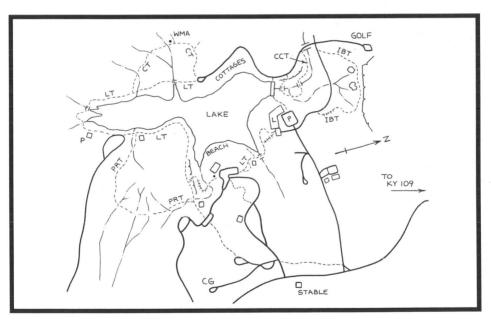

PENNYRILE FOREST STATE RESORT PARK

Lake Trail Loop (1.75 miles). Those desiring a shorter hike can follow the **Lake Trail** as it negotiates the shoreline of Pennyrile Lake. From the west side of the Lodge, the trail descends to the Dam, crosses it, and then uses a section of the Cottage Road as it climbs above the western shore. Continue around the Lake, crosses numerous inlets and bypassing cutoffs to the **Cane** and **Pennyroyal Trails**. The loop eventually passes the Beach area and returns to the east side of the Lodge.

7 HIGGINSON-HENRY WILDLIFE MANAGEMENT AREA

Distance: Day hikes of 1.5 to 6.4 miles
Terrain: hilly
Walking time: 1.5 to 4.5 hours

Adventurous hikers may want to explore the forested hills of the **Higginson-Henry Wildlife Management Area**, southeast of Morganfield. Spreading across the rugged terrain of the Sulphur Spring Hills, this preserve is best known for Cap Mauzy Lake, a popular destination for area fishermen.

Most of the Wildlife Management Area is covered by second or third growth hardwood forest and the Sulphur Spring Hills are dissected by numerous streams. A wide path, just over 3 miles in length, follows the ridgetop, from Cap Mauzy Lake to an old lookout tower (T). This path can be accessed from several parking areas within the refuge (see map).

Directions: The Wildlife Management Area stretches along the south side of Ky 56, southeast of Morganfield. The turnoff to Cap Mauzy Lake is 5.2 miles from the city limits; other distances, in miles, are noted on the map.

Routes: As noted above, a wide path follows the ridgetop of the Sulphur Spring Hills. Access to the trail is via parking areas just west of the Mauzy Lake dam, at the lookout tower (T) or at road crossings, as illustrated on the map. Elevations range from 430 feet at the base of the hills to 673 feet at the lookout tower; the ridgetop elevation averages 550-600 feet.

We suggest the following day hikes:

Ky 758 crossing to Lookout Tower - 1.5 miles roundtrip
Cap Mauzy Lake to Lookout Tower - 6.4 miles roundtrip
Cap Mauzy Lake to Ky 758 crossing - 4.9 miles roundtrip

*Crossing the
Sulphur Spring Hills*

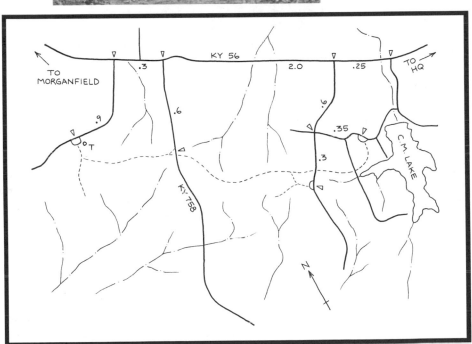

HIGGINSON-HENRY WILDLIFE MANAGEMENT AREA

8 SAUERHEBER WILDLIFE REFUGE

Distance: 3.4 miles roundtrip
Terrain: flat
Walking time: 2 hours

Part of the Sloughs Wildlife Management Area, the **Sauerheber Wildlife Refuge** is a 3000 acre preserve, northwest of Geneva, Kentucky. Open to hunters and naturalists from March 16 to October 14, the refuge is closed to the public the remainder of the year, providing important wintering habitat for more than 35,000 geese and 10,000 ducks; bald eagles also winter here.

Visitors during the spring, summer and early fall will find a superb variety of wildlife at the **Sauerheber Refuge.** White-tailed deer, raccoons, quail, herons, egrets and numerous songbirds inhabit the preserve, as do a fine collection of snakes, turtles and amphibians. Birdwatchers should plan to visit in April to catch the tide of migrant shorebirds that stop to rest and feed on the flooded fields.

Directions: From Henderson, proceed west on U.S. 60 for approximately 5.8 miles. Bear right onto Ky 136 and drive 2.7 miles, to the town of Geneva. Take Ky 268 northwest from Geneva and proceed 6.2 miles to the refuge, on your left.

Route: Park near the refuge buildings (see map) and hike southward along the gravel road that parallels a large baldcypress swamp. Scan the open waters for wood ducks, blue-winged teal and other waterfowl. Herons, egrets, frogs and turtles may be spotted along the shore while kingfishers and red-headed woodpeckers dart among the trees.

Once past the cypress swamp, the road curves eastward, crossing open fields where seasonal flooding attracts shorebirds, mallards and teal. Such open country is also a good place to watch for birds of prey; red-tailed hawks, kestrels and northern harriers are common here and rough-legged hawks may be spotted in early spring. Though bald eagles are most abundant in winter, when the refuge is closed, a few nest at the preserve and may be seen soaring overhead.

Continue out to the end of the gravel road and then return to your car via the same route. Your roundtrip walking distance will total 3.4 miles.

*Flooded fields attract migrant shorebirds
and waterfowl to the refuge*

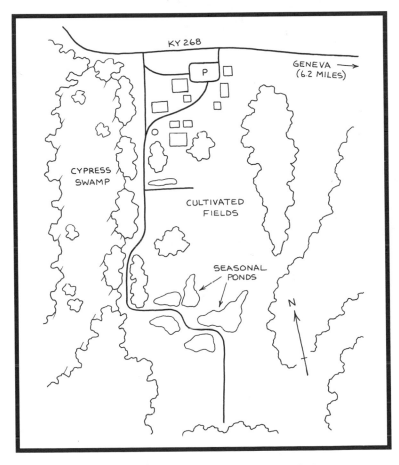

SAUERHEBER WILDLIFE REFUGE

V. HIKING AREAS OF WEST-CENTRAL KENTUCKY

9. John James Audubon State Park

10. Yellowbank Wildlife Management Area

11. Otter Creek Park

12. Jefferson Memorial Forest

13. Rough River Dam State Resort Park

14. Freeman Lake

15. Mammoth Cave National Park

16. Lake Malone State Park

17. Logan County Glade Nature Preserve

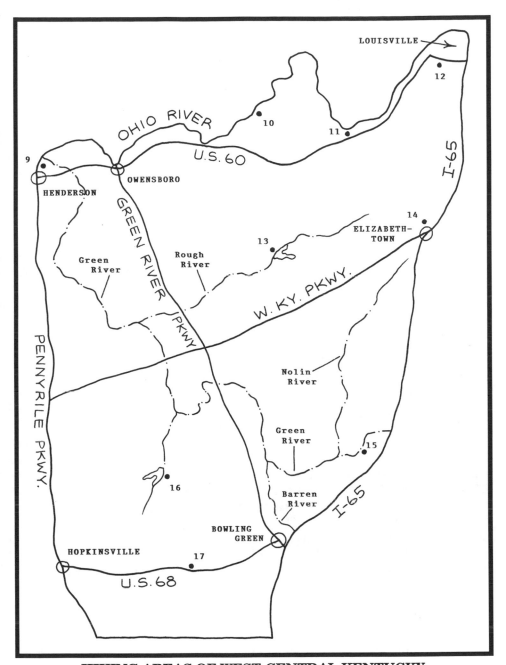

HIKING AREAS OF WEST-CENTRAL KENTUCKY

9 JOHN JAMES AUDUBON STATE PARK

Combined Loop Hike
  Distance: 3.6 miles
  Terrain: hilly
  Walking time: 2 hours

John James Audubon, the renowned painter and naturalist, moved to Louisville, Kentucky, soon after his marriage in April, 1808. There, he and his wife, Lucy, ran a general supply store. More enamored with the countryside than with the inside of a mercantile, Audubon gave up his business pursuits and moved on to Henderson. It was here that he began work on his famous *Birds of America* paintings and he remained in the area for the next ten years.

John James Audubon State Park, just north of Henderson, pays tribute to this early American naturalist and preserves the rich, deciduous forest that inspired much of his original work. The Park's museum (M), recently renovated, houses a collection of Audubon's paintings.

Directions: The Park stretches east from U.S. 41, just south of the Ohio River bridge, between Henderson, Kentucky, and Evansville, Indiana. Park near the office (P.O.) and museum (M).

Route: Eight hiking trails provide access to the Park's forest preserve. We suggest the following loop, which yields a hike of approximately 3.6 miles.

From the Park Office, hike northeastward along the **Warbler Road (WR)** which climbs steadily through the rich, hardwood forest. Birdlife is plentiful here; wood thrushes, warblers, vireos and pewees fill the woods with song during the summer months while pileated woodpeckers, chickadees and nuthatches roam the forest throughout the year. Bypass cutoffs to the **King Benson (KBT)** and **Lake Overlooks (LOT) Trails**, dip across two drainages and, as the **Warbler Road** curves to the west, turn right on to the **Back Country Trail (BCT)**. This 1.6 mile trail passes an old stone fireplace (F), crosses numerous drainages and runs atop a low ridge which yields a view of the Ohio River and the U.S. 41 bridge.

The **Back Country Trail** eventually descends to the shore of **Wilderness Lake** where it intersects the **Wilderness Lake Trail (WLT)**. Turn left, hugging the north shore of this woodland oasis and crossing several inlets. Watch for green-backed herons, wood ducks and red-bellied woodpeckers as you skirt the wetland. Climbing eastward, the trail leads to the end of the **Warbler Road (WR)**. Backtrack along this roadway to the **Lake Overlooks Trail (LOT)** and turn right; within .2 mile you will reach a multi-trail intersection.

Angle onto the **Ky. Coffeetree Trail (KCT)** which descends atop a side ridge and then turns eastward to cross a stream. Turn right and ascend to the **Museum (M)** area via either path (see map).

Wilderness Lake

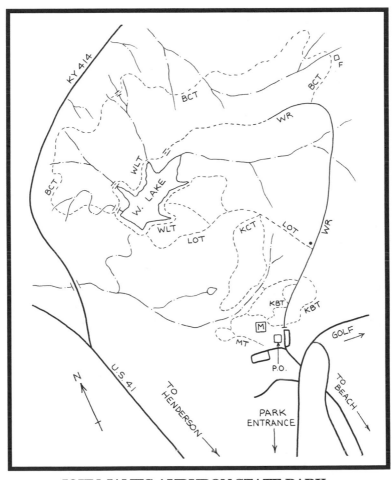

JOHN JAMES AUDUBON STATE PARK

39

10 YELLOWBANK WILDLIFE MANAGEMENT AREA

Loop 1
 Distance: 3 miles
 Terrain: rolling, some hills
 Walking time: 2 hours

Loop 2
 Distance: 6 miles
 Terrain: rolling, some hills
 Walking time: 4 hours

Those who venture into wildlife management areas soon learn that these open spaces do not offer the manicured trails and "comfort facilities" of the State Parks. Indeed, most of these areas occupy reclaimed strip mines, naturalized farmlands or reforested timber tracts. Yet, for adventurous wanderers, wildlife management areas provide a welcome escape from the "developed" parklands so inviting to the golf and picnic crowd.

Yellowbank Wildlife Management Area, almost 18 miles north of Hardinsburg, is an appealing destination for naturalists. Stretching along the east bank of the Ohio River, the preserve is divided into four tracts which are partly separated by private land holdings. Tract 1, near the River, is covered by floodplain woodlands, crop fields and riverside marsh. Tracts 2-4 spread uphill from Ky 259; characterized by upland meadows, old farm ponds and parcels of hardwood forest, these sections are accessed by the hikes described below.

Directions: From U.S. 60 in Hardinsburg, head north on Ky 259. Drive 17.7 miles and you will reach the check station (CS) for the Yellowbank Wildlife Management Area. Proceed to parking areas P1 or P2 (our terminology), as illustrated on the map; sectional road mileages are shown.

Routes: Access to the refuge is via a network of gravel roads and jeep trails, most of which are closed to motorized vehicles. We suggest the following day hikes.

Loop 1. This 3 mile route begins at lot 2 (P2). Hike southward from the lot and turn right at the first intersection, passing an old farm pond. Wind to the SSE, eventually crossing a creek, and turn left, paralleling the stream until it enters Yellowbank Creek (YBC). Recross the sidestream, hike to the NNW and turn right at the next intersection. This trail soon crosses a drainage, passes an old structure and leads across a wooded meadow to a roadway. Turn left and hike along the road for .7 mile to the parking lot access lane (see map).

Loop 2. This 6 mile route departs from the access road to lot 1 (P1). After curving southward to cross a drainage, the path angles to the ENE. Bear left at the first two intersections, eventually crossing two streams and heading northward. The path soon merges with another trail and descends toward Yellowbank Creek (YBC). Turn right on the trail that parallels the Creek (see map), bypass cutoffs to the east and cross Yellowbank Creek near its junction with Flint Run.

After hiking along Flint Run for a short distance, turn west (left) on the

*A typical scene at
Yellowbank*

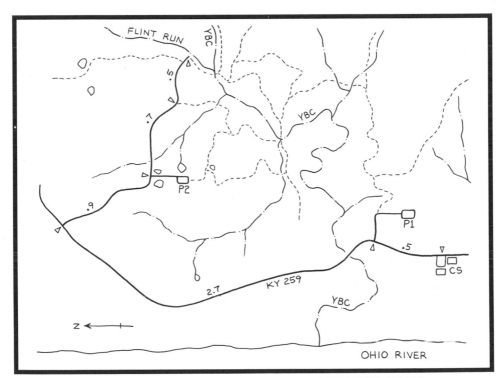

YELLOWBANK WILDLIFE MANAGEMENT AREA

roadway, walk .5 mile and turn left on an old jeep trail that leads south-ward across a meadow. Pass an old structure, cross a stream and turn left at the next intersection. After crossing another stream near its junction with Yellowbank Creek, turn left and ford Yellowbank Creek (YBC) itself. Bear right at the next four intersections, eventually reaching the P1 access road.

11 OTTER CREEK PARK

Blue Trail
  Distance: 8.1 miles
  Terrain: hilly
  Walking time: 6 hrs.

Yellow Trail
  Distance: 3.7 miles
  Terrain: hilly
  Walking time: 3 hrs.

Red Trail
  Distance: 2.7 miles
  Terrain: rolling
  Walking time: 2 hrs.

Otter Creek Park, owned and operated by the city of Louisville, sprawls atop a wooded plateau at the confluence of Otter Creek and the Ohio River. Rugged cliffs, scenic overlooks and streamside paths make this 3600-acre Park an excellent destination for hikers. Indeed, over 15 miles of hiking trails criss-cross the plateau and descend to the west bank of Otter Creek.

Directions: From the west end of I-265 (KY 841) in southwest Louisville, head SSW on U.S.60/31W. Drive 13 miles and turn right (west) on Ky1638. The Park entrance will be 1.6 miles, on your right. A nominal day-use fee is charged for parking at picnic areas on Otter Creek and at lots near the Ohio River. Trails are best accessed from lots at or near the Nature Center (NC).

Routes: There are three primary trail loops at Otter Creek Park; since they interconnect atop the plateau, hikers can plan a variety of routes, using one or more of the major trails (see map).
    Blue Trail (BT). This is the longest trail at Otter Creek Park, covering 8.1 miles as it circumnavigates the central plateau. The western section of route parallels the main Park road, crossing open woodlands and meadows. Near the Park entrance, the **Blue Trail** angles to the east and descends to Otter Creek which it follows downstream toward its junction with the Ohio River. After undulating across numerous drainages, the trail finally climbs back on to the plateau, joining the **Red Trail (RT)** for a final excursion above the cliffs.
    Yellow Trail (YT). Beginning at the Nature Center (NC), this 3.7 mile loop cuts directly eastward to the Otter Creek valley where it turns northward for a strenuous journey along the east wall of the plateau. The trail descends through a scenic gorge before climbing back to join the **Red Trail**. Turn left at this junction and follow the yellow blazes back to the Nature Center.
    Red Trail (RT). This is the shortest (2. 7 miles) and easiest hiking trail at Otter Creek Park. Its loop section (approximately 2.2 miles) crosses rolling terrain atop the plateau, sharing part of its route with the **Blue Trail** and **Yellow Trail**. Those who pick up the **Red Trail** from parking lots along the Ohio River must first endure a steep, .5 mile climb to the loop; less energetic hikers may want to begin at the Nature Center (NC) and hike northeastward on the **Yellow Trail** to access the **Red Trail** loop.

A summer day on Otter Creek

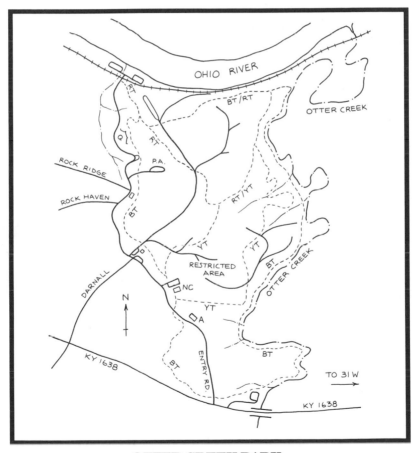

OTTER CREEK PARK

Tom Wallace Combined Loop
Distance: 3 miles
Terrain: hilly
Walking time: 2 hours

Siltstone Trail
Distance: 6.5 miles (one way)
Terrain: hilly
Walking time: 4.0-4.5 hours

Mitch McConnell Loop
Distance: 2.9-6.4 miles
Terrain: hilly
Walking time: 2.0-4.5 hours

Scotts Gap Loop Trail
Distance: 4 miles
Terrain: hilly
Walking time: 2.5 hours

A chain of forested hills stretches east to west, some twelve miles south of downtown Louisville. **Jefferson County Memorial Forest** cloaks 5128 acres along the crest of this ridge, offering a natural wonderland for campers, horsemen, hikers and other outdoor enthusiasts. Over 22 miles of trails lace the Forest and a new Welcome Center (WC), located on Mitchell Hill Road, introduces visitors to the human history of the area.

All hiking trails within Jefferson County Memorial Forest will eventually interconnect at the Welcome Center. For now, hikers should plan their excursions from one of three areas: the **Tom Wallace Area**, the **Paul Yost Area** or the **Scotts Gap Trailhead**.

Directions: To reach the **Tom Wallace** and **Paul Yost Areas**, take Exit 6 from I-265/KY 841 (the Gene Snyder Freeway). Head south on KY 1865 (which becomes KY 2055). Drive 1.4 miles and turn right on Mitchell Hill Road. Proceed .9 mile to a junction where Holsclaw Hill Road angles to the left. From this junction, the **Paul Yost Area** is .5 mile via Holsclaw Hill Road while the **Tom Wallace Area** and **Welcome Center** are .6 mile via Mitchell Hill Road (see map).

To reach the **Scotts Gap Trailhead**, take Exit 3 from I-265/KY 841 and head south on Stonestreet Road. Proceed .6 mile and continue south on Blevins Gap Road. Another 2.1 miles bring you to Scotts Gap Road; turn left and drive .9 mile to the trailhead parking lot, on your right. The lot is open for use from 8AM to 4:30PM, daily.

Routes: **SCOTTS GAP TRAILHEAD**

Scotts Gap Loop Trail (4 miles) From the parking lot off Scotts Gap Road, climb to the **Loop Trail** via an access path (see map). Follow the loop clockwise, heading westward and crossing numerous drainages. A half-mile from the trailhead, the route angles to the south, following one of the larger creeks downstream. After turning westward once again, watch for a sharp turn to the right (*). The trail soon passes an abandoned car (C) and, after negotiating a series of low ridges and ravines, turns northward through a wide stream valley.

*Atop a ridge in
Jefferson County
Memorial Forest*

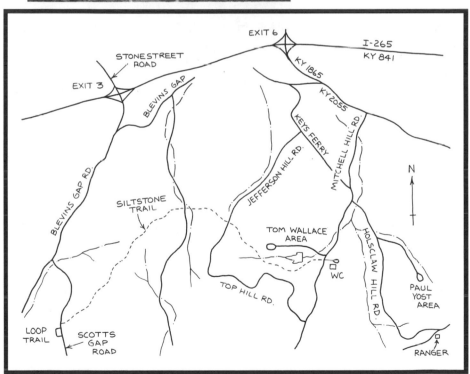

JEFFERSON COUNTY MEMORIAL FOREST

Nearing the upper reaches of this drainage, the trail cuts away from the creek and climbs to the northwest. The path now turns eastward and levels out atop the ridge, yielding broad views during the "leafless" months of the year. Two overlooks (V) are especially rewarding. Bypass the short-cut "connector trail" and begin a winding descent to the trailhead area. Before reaching your original entry path, you will pass the western terminus of the **Siltstone Trail (SST)**, discussed below.

TOM WALLACE AREA

Tom Wallace Combined Loop (3 miles). From the first parking lot off the entry road to the Tom Wallace Area, hike northward on a trail that climbs on to a ridge and turns westward atop its crest (see map). Bypass cut-off paths that descend either side of the ridge, continuing straight ahead until the trail ends at an intersection.

Turn left, descend a short distance and then angle left on the **Siltstone Trail (SST)**. A broad switchback brings you down to a streamside shelter where the paved **Tulip Tree Trail (TT)** leads back to a group picnic area.

Stay on the **Siltstone Trail**, climbing on to the opposite ridge and then hiking eastward atop its crest. Bypass a steep side trail to the dam crossing and begin a gradual, winding descent to your original trailhead.

Siltstone Trail (SST; 6.5 miles one way). By using two cars, or by enduring a 13-mile roundtrip dayhike, hikers can follow this well-engineered trail from the Welcome Center (WC), on Mitchell Hill Road, to the Scotts Gap Trailhead. From the Welcome Center, the **Siltstone Trail** ascends on to a ridge and heads westward above the Lake at the Tom Wallace Area. After descending to ford the Lake's feeder stream, the Trail climbs on to the next ridge where it crosses Jefferson Hill Road. A second valley descent is followed by a long ridgetop excursion to the Scotts Gap Trailhead (see the overview map)

PAUL YOST AREA

Mitch McConnell Loop Trail. Located off Holsclaw Hill Road, the Paul Yost Area serves as a trailhead for a vast network of hiking and bridle trails. The **Mitch McConnell Loop Trail**, limited to foot travel, is actually a double loop; the **Blue Trail (BT)** is 2.9 miles long while the **Yellow Trail (YT)** is 6.0 miles. Since these two loop interconnect (as is evident on the map), one can plan a variety of loop hikes, ranging in distance from 1.3 to 6.0 miles. Indeed, a marker at the trailhead outlines the possible routes.

The rugged topography at Paul Yost (steep ridges and deep ravines) makes for rather strenuous hiking; distances will seem to be considerably longer than the trail signs indicate. We recommend this area for fit and experienced trekkers!

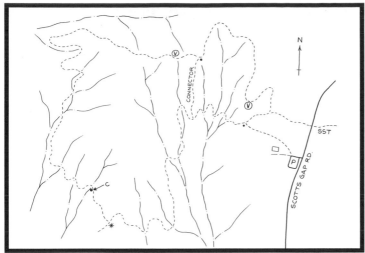

SCOTTS GAP LOOP TRAIL

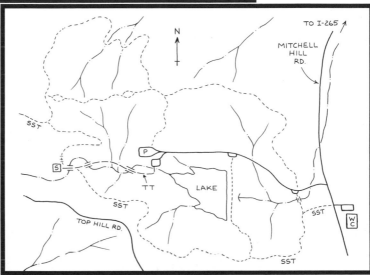

TOM WALLACE AREA

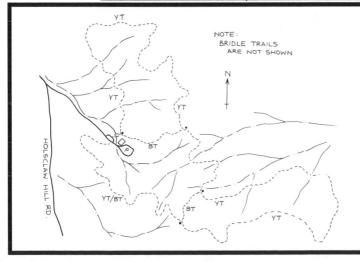

MITCH McCONNELL LOOP

47

13 ROUGH RIVER DAM STATE RESORT PARK

Lakeshore Nature Trail
  Distance: 1.8 miles roundtrip
  Terrain: rolling
  Walking time: 1.5 hours

Folklore Nature Trail
  Distance: 1 mile
  Terrain: rolling
  Walking time: .75 hour

Designed for flood control, water supply and recreational use, Rough River Dam was constructed between 1955 and 1961 by the Louisville District of the U.S. Army Corps of Engineers. The **State Resort Park**, which stretches along the Lake's western shore, near the Dam, offers two hiking trails.

Directions: From the Western Kentucky Parkway, take Exit 94 and head north on Ky 79. The Park entrance will be 14.7 miles ahead, on your right.

Routes: As mentioned above, there are two hiking trails at Rough River Dam State Resort Park.

Lakeshore Nature Trail (NT). This .9 mile path (1.8 miles roundtrip), begins at a boat dock behind and below the Lodge. It then snakes southward above the western shore of Rough River Lake, crossing several drainages along the way. Near its halfway point, the trail splits for a short distance (see map); footing is better on the upper fork.

Continue southward along the main trail, soon passing a number of cottages. The trail ends above an inlet, near the Park's marina. Return to the Lodge via the same route, completing a roundtrip hike of 1.8 miles.

Folklore Trail (FNT). This short (1 mile) but interesting hike begins at a parking lot on the west side of Ky 79, just south of the Dam. A brochure, available at the trailhead, guides visitors along the woodland path where 27 numbered stations highlight the natural and cultural history of the region. Among the more interesting features are an old cabin (C) and a natural spring (S). The trail itself is a well-engineered loop which uses a series of fine wooden bridges to cross the woodland's numerous streams.

Late summer at Rough River Lake

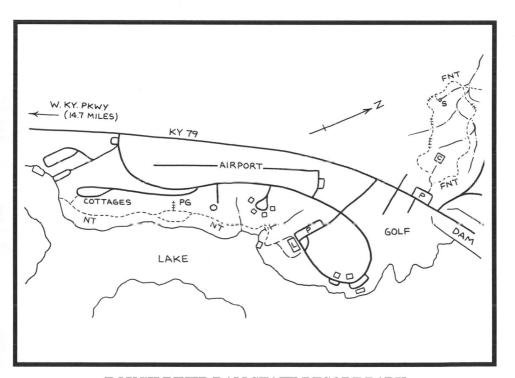

ROUGH RIVER DAM STATE RESORT PARK

14 FREEMAN LAKE

Freeman Lake Trail
  Distance: 4.8 miles
  Terrain: rolling
  Walking time: 3 hours

Freeman Lake/Pirtle Center Loop
  Distance: 5.3 miles
  Terrain: rolling
  Walking time: 3.5 hours

John Helm/Freeman Lake Loop
  Distance: 6.3 miles
  Terrain: rolling
  Walking time: 4.0-4.5 hours

Established in 1974, **Greenspace Inc.** is a nonprofit corporation, created to promote, develop and manage the Greenbelt Park network throughout the city of Elizabethtown. While short walking paths are found throughout the system, serious hikers will be most interested in the trails surrounding **Freeman Lake**, north of the downtown area.

Directions: From downtown Elizabethtown, head north on U.S. 31W. Drive 2 miles to the Freeman Lake Park entrance road, on your right. Hikers can park here or at lots on Ring Road (north of the Lake), at the Pirtle Center Trailhead (PC) on Pear Orchard Road, or at Helmwood Plaza, one mile south of the Lake (see map).

Routes: By parking in one of the lots described above, one can easily access the **Freeman Lake Trail (FLT)**, which makes a 4.8 mile circuit around the Lake. Along the west shore, the Trail crosses open meadows and Park lawns, where its route is blazed with metal posts. East of the Lake, the path winds along the edge of a forest, curving eastward to cross inlet streams (see map).

Those who park at **Pirtle Center (PC)**, on Pear Orchard Road, will add a .5 mile forest loop to their hike, bringing the total distance to 5.3 miles. Longer yet is the combined hike from the **Helmwood Plaza** lot, on the east side of U.S. 31W, one mile south of the Lake. The **John Helm Trail**, paved south of Diecks Drive, follows Freeman Creek for 3/4 mile, intersecting the **Freeman Lake Trail** below the dam; the combined, roundtrip hike along the **John Helm** and **Freeman Lake Trails** is thus 6.3 miles.

Scene on the Braddock Creek inlet

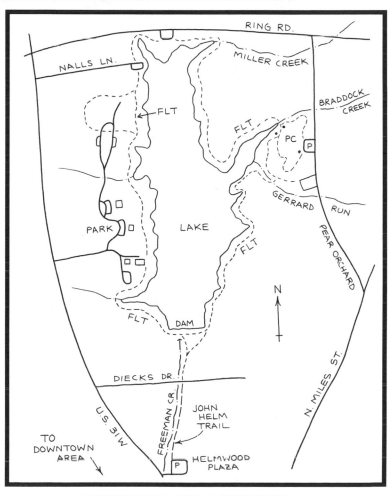

FREEMAN LAKE & VICINITY

15 MAMMOTH CAVE NATIONAL PARK

Distance: Variable; day hikes of .6 to 8.6 miles suggested
Terrain: hilly (except Heritage Trail)
Walking time: Variable; walks of .5 to 6 hours suggested

Protected by a roof of sandstone, the limestone tunnels and caverns of **Mammoth Cave National Park** comprise the largest known system of caves on the planet. The limestone itself, deposited in Mississippian seas over 300 million years ago, has been hollowed out by underground streams during the past 2 million years. Fissures in the overlying sandstone permit some surface water to percolate down through the limestone, opening vertical shafts and yielding classic features of the subterranean world: stalactites, stalagmites and flowstones.

While these fabulous caves attract visitors from across the globe, **Mammoth Cave National Park** also offers a superb variety of hiking trails for "topside" explorers. Indeed, over 70 miles of hiking and bridal paths yield access to the varied habitats of the Park. We have grouped these trails into three regions: the **Visitor Center Area**, the **Back-Country Area** and **Outlying Trails.**

Directions: From I-65, take Exit 53 and head west on Ky 70. When nearing the Park boundary, angle northward on Ky 255 for the shortest route to the **Visitor Center (VC)/Hotel (H)/ Lodge (L) Area** (see overview map on next page).

Hikers should proceed to one of the following Trailheads:

Visitor Center (VC) - access to the Heritage Trail, the Green River Bluffs Trail, the Cave Island Nature Trail and the Echo River Trail.

Maple Springs Road (MSR) - access to the Raymer Hollow, Sal Hollow and Ganter Cave Trails.

Good Spring Church (GSC) - access to Good Spring Loop Trail and Turnhole Bend Trail.

Lincoln Trailhead (LT) - access to Collie Ridge Trail and connectors.

Temple Hill Cemetery (THC) - access to First Hollow Creek Trail and the McCoy Hollow Trail.

Houchins Ferry Road (HFR) - this trail crossing area, 3.6 miles north of the Temple Hill Cemetery, yields access to the First Hollow Creek Trail and the Wet Prong Trail.

View from the Green River Bluffs Trail

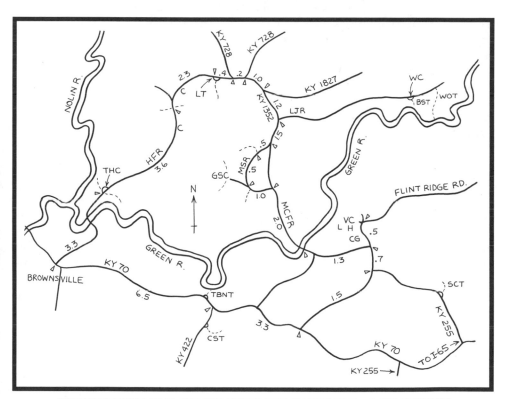

OVERVIEW MAP OF MAMMOTH CAVE N.P. & VICINITY

Routes: The extensive trail network at **Mammoth Cave National Park** offers a tremendous variety of potential day hikes. We have grouped the trails within three regions and suggest day hikes within each area.

THE VISITOR CENTER AREA

Novice hikers and those planning a quick trek between cave tours should proceed to this area. The trails are relatively short, well-engineered and close to "comfort facilities." Sectional mileages are indicated on the map (next page).

We suggest the following day hikes:

Heritage Trail (HT). This .6 mile loop hike begins and ends at the Park Hotel (H). The trail is graded and, using a series of boardwalks, leads westward to **Sunset Point (SP)** which overlooks the Green River Valley. Plan .5 hour for this casual stroll.

Cave Island Nature Trail (CINT). This 1.4 mile loop begins and ends near a cave entrance, a short distance west of the Visitor Center (see map). The northern arm climbs across a ridge before descending to the Green River while the southern arm follows a wide, graded path. A short side trail at the west end of the loop leads down to the **River Styx Spring (RS)**. Plan at least 1 hour for this hike.

Green River Bluffs Trail (GRBT)-Echo River Trail (ERT) Loop (3.9 miles). Pick up the **Green River Bluffs Trail** along a paved road that leads NNW from the Visitor Center parking lot (see map). This .8 mile trail loops around a forested knob, passing rock cliffs and offering several viewpoints (V) along the way. Nearing the Green River, it intersects the **Cave Island Nature Trail (CINT)**; bear right and continue southward to the **River Styx Spring (RS).**

From the Spring, pick up the .2 mile connector trail that leads upward and eastward to the **Echo River Trail (ERT)**. Continue southward on this path which parallels the Green River, curving eastward to cross several creek beds. At the **Echo River Spring (ERS)**, the **Echo River Trail** cuts back to the northeast, climbing past rock outcroppings. Bypass the **Campgrounds Trail (CGT)** and you will soon reach **White's Cave (WC)**, a 200 foot long tunnel in the limestone bedrock; the cave is closed to the public.

The **Echo River Trail** climbs higher via a broad switchback and soon passes **Mammoth Dome Sink (MD)** where a cave has collapsed to form a large depression. Angling the to north, the main trail continues its gradual ascent, crossing the valley wall and eventually intersecting the **Heritage Trail (HT)**. Turn right for a short stroll back to the Hotel (H) and Visitor Center (VC). Your combined hike has totalled 3.9 miles; plan 2-2.5 hours for this excursion.

The River Styx Spring

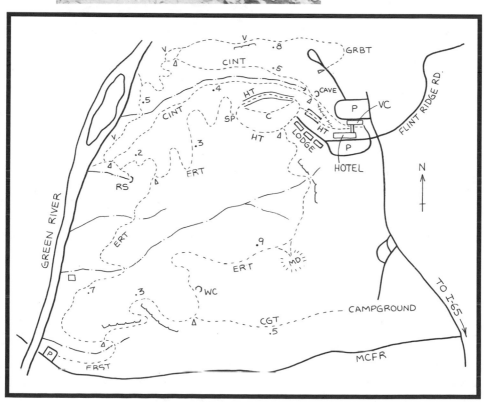

THE VISITOR CENTER AREA

A superb network of back-country trails and back-country campgrounds will be found north of the Green River and west of the Visitor Center Area. The trails lead across hilly terrain, bounded by the Nolin River to the west and the Green River to the south and east. The ridge-valley topography has been sculpted by a vast network of streams, the most prominant of which are Wet Prong (WPC) and Dry Prong (DPC) Creeks. Sectional trail mileages are noted on the map (next page); for a more detailed discussion of these back-country trails, we suggest that you refer to *A Guide to Surface Trails of Mammoth Cave National Park*, by Stanley D. Sides (see Bibliography).

Good Spring Loop Trail (7 miles). Perhaps the most popular day hike in the Park's back-country, this loop begins and ends at **Good Spring Church (GSC)**, a United Baptist Church founded in 1842. The Loop Trail encircles a section of the Dry Prong valley, using a 1 mile portion of the **Collie Ridge Trail (CRT)** along its western arm. The route may be hiked in either direction and provides access to other back-country trails: the **Turnhole Bend Trail (TBT)**, the west end of the **Sal Hollow Trail (SHT)**, the **Collie Ridge Trail (CRT)** and the east end of the **McCoy Hollow Trail (MHT).** Plan at least 4 hours to complete the **Good Spring Loop Trail**.

Good Spring Church to Turnhole Bend (3.2 miles roundtrip). This hike begins at the Good Spring Church (GSC). Pick up the south arm of the **Good Spring Loop Trail (GSLT)**, hike .6 mile and turn left (south) on the **Turnhole Bend Trail (TBT)** which leads down to the Green River. A short distance beyond the **Sal Hollow Trail (SHT)** intersection you are treated to a spectacular view of the Green River Valley. Thereafter, the trail begins a steep descent to the River's north bank. Plan at least 2 hours for this roundtrip hike.

Maple Spring Road (MSR) to Ganter Cave (3.6 miles roundtrip). This hike begins along Maple Spring Road, .8 mile west of Mammoth Cave Ferry Road (see map). Hike southward along the **Sal Hollow Trail (SHT)**; just over 1 mile from the trailhead you will reach Fishtrap Hollow where the path forks. Turn left on the **Ganter Cave Trail (GCT)** which descends along the creek bed to the Green River; the Cave, closed to the public, is a short distance downstream. Plan at least 2 hours for this roundtrip hike.

Lincoln Trailhead (LT) to Good Spring Church (8.6 miles roundtrip). This hike begins at the Lincoln Trailhead, 5.9 miles north of the Temple Hill Cemetery, on Houchins Ferry Road; this site is .4 mile west of the Ky 728 junction.

Hike southward on the **Collie Ridge Trail (CRT)** which follows high ground between the Wet Prong Creek (WPC) and Dry Prong Creek (DPC) basins. Three miles south of the trailhead, cut eastward on the north arm of the **Good Spring Loop Trail (GSLT)**, which dips through the Dry Prong and

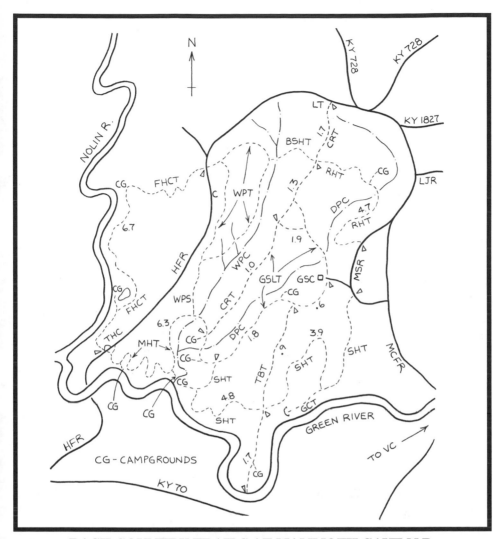

BACK-COUNTRY TRAILS AT MAMMOTH CAVE N.P.

then climbs to the **Good Spring Church (GSC)**. Plan at least 6 hours for this long excursion.

Wet Prong Trail (WPT; 5 miles). This hike begins and ends on the east side of Houchins Ferry Road, 3.6 miles northeast of the Temple Hill Cemetery (THC). Hike eastward and bear left at the fork, descending toward Wet Prong Creek (WPC). Bypass the **Blair Spring Hollow Trail (BSHT)**, remaining on the **Wet Prong Trail** which turns southward to parallel the Creek. After crossing numerous sidestreams the trail curves to the west where the **Wet Prong Spur Trail (WPS)** intersects the loop. Bypass this trail and continue on the **Wet Prong Trail**, hiking northward to the trailhead. Plan 3 hours for this loop hike.

OUTLYING TRAILS

While most of the hiking trails at Mammoth Cave National Park are located near the Visitor Center or within the Back-Country Area, there are several trails in outlying sections of the Park that deserve mention:

Cedar Sink Trail (CST). This 1 mile trail (2 miles roundtrip) begins on the east side of Ky 422, .6 mile south of Ky 70 (see map). After winding through the forest, the trail descends into **Cedar Sink**, a large basin formed by the collapse of a cave system. Water from this subterranean network still wells up on the floor of the sink, producing a series of ponds. Cave openings will also be spotted along the steep walls of the sink.

Turnhole Bend Nature Trail (TBNT). Also 1 mile in length (2 miles roundtrip), this trail begins on the north side of Ky 70, just west of the Ky 422 junction (see overview map). The upper section of the route forms a loop which passes a series of sinkholes while the lower section leads down to the **Blue Hole Spring**, on the south bank of the Green River.

Sand Cave Trail (SCT). This short trail (.5 mile roundtrip) begins on the east side of Ky 255, just north of the Park boundary (see overview map). The path leads out to the entrance of Sand Cave, made famous in 1925 when Floyd Collins became trapped (and died) in the cave.

Big Spring Trail (BST). This path, .8 mile roundtrip, leads from the Wilkins Cemetery (WC), on Little Jordan Road (LJR) to an overlook above the Green River Valley (see overview map).

White Oak Trail (WOT). This strenuous hike, 5.5 miles roundtrip, begins along Little Jordan Road (see overview map). Following the old Dennison Ferry Road, the trail leads out to the edge of the Green River gorge and then drops 400 feet to the north bank of the River.

The Good Spring Church

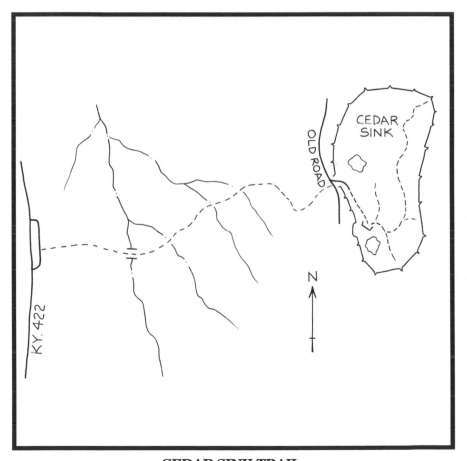

CEDAR SINK TRAIL

16 LAKE MALONE STATE PARK

Combined Loop Hike
Distance: 2.2 miles
Terrain: rolling; some hills
Walking time: 1.5 hours

Most reservoirs, being unnatural creations of man, are rimmed by seasonal mudflats and drowned woodlands. Not so Lake Malone, a scenic, 788-acre lake west of Dunmor, Kentucky. Sheer rock walls, composed primarily of Mississippian sandstone, rise 50-200 feet above the shimmering water.

Long a popular destination for fishermen, the reservoir is now home to **Lake Malone State Park**, which stretches along its northern shore. The Park offers lake access, campgrounds, picnic sites and a scenic, lakeside path, the **Laurel Trail (LT)**.

Directions: From the Western Kentucky Parkway, exit at Central City and head south on U.S. 431. Drive 16.8 miles to Dunmor and turn right (west) on Ky 973. Proceed another 3.4 miles to the Park entrance road (which is .7 mile beyond the dam) and turn left. Follow this road for 1 mile to a large parking lot above the Lake's north shore (see map).

Route: The Park's nature trail, the **Laurel Trail (LT)** yields a pleasant, 1.5 mile hike above the Lake's northern shore. By combining this path with a return route, described below, the visitor can achieve a loop hike of 2.2 miles.

The **Laurel Trail** leaves the southwest end of the parking lot, heading westward above the north shore of Lake Malone, and soon forks; bear right, climbing through outcroppings of sandstone. A side path leads out to an overlook atop this Carboniferous rock while the main trail, blazed with blue and white paint, curves northward to cross an inlet stream.

Continuing toward the west, the trail hugs the edge of the rock wall where white pines and beech trees have sunk their roots into these ancient sea sediments. Further along, the **Laurel Trail** curves northward above a beautiful, rock-walled cove and soon climbs to the rim of the lake basin. Paralleling the edge of a field, the trail finally exits the mixed hardwood-pine forest and ends.

Turn left (east) along the northern edge of the field, soon passing the Park Office (P.O.). Angle to the southeast and proceed to a roadway that runs along a wooded picnic area (P.A.). Follow this lane to the main Park road and turn right for a gradual descent to the parking lot.

*Rock ledges along
the Laurel Trail*

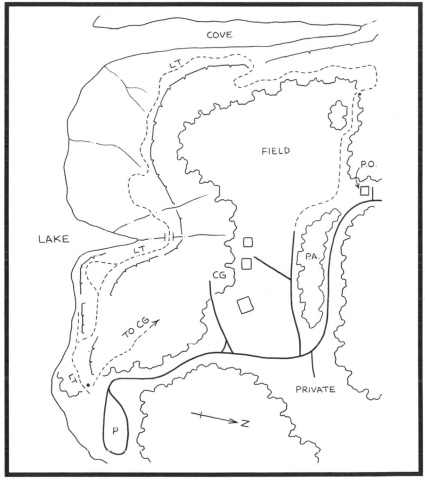

LAKE MALONE STATE PARK

17 LOGAN COUNTY GLADE NATURE PRESERVE

Distance: 1 mile
Terrain: hilly
Walking time: .75 hour

Before white settlers arrived in southwest Kentucky, extensive prairies covered much of the karst plain. Thin soil and subsurface limestone hindered the invasion of forest, allowing hardy grasslands to spread across the "Big Barrens." These prairie ecosystems eventually succumbed to the farmer's plow but grassland remnants still persist on steep, south-facing hillsides where steady erosion, rocky soil and solar evaporation have kept the forest at bay.

One such prairie remnant is protected within the **Logan County Glade Nature Preserve**, on the edge of Russellville. This 41 acre preserve, dedicated in January, 1991, honors J. Granville Clark who inspired its creation. A 1-mile trail loop provides access to the prairie remnant and surrounding forest.

Directions: The Nature Preserve is on the southeast edge of Russellville, just behind the old Hospital building (H). When coming west on U.S. 68 from Bowling Green, proceed .3 mile beyond the Ky 100 junction and turn right on E. 5th St. A graveled lot , servicing the Preserve, will be on your right, near the bend in the road (see map).

Route: A plaque, at the trailhead, describes the natural history of the Preserve and its dedication to J. Granville Clark. Enter the hillside forest and follow the path as it curves to the southeast. You will soon arrive at the edge of the largest prairie remnant; characterized by Indian grass, big bluestem and little bluestem, the grassland is adorned with wildflowers throughout the warmer months. Redbud and cedar, common pioneers in forest clearings, are slowly invading the prairie, which, if left undisturbed, will eventually yield to the hardwood forest.

Bear left at the fork in the trail, skirting the edge of the grassland and then climbing higher across the forested ridge. After crossing several drainages, the trail turns westward, descending via a series of switchbacks. It then enters a second prairie remnant , angles to the northwest and leads back to the entry area (see map).

62

April at the Glade

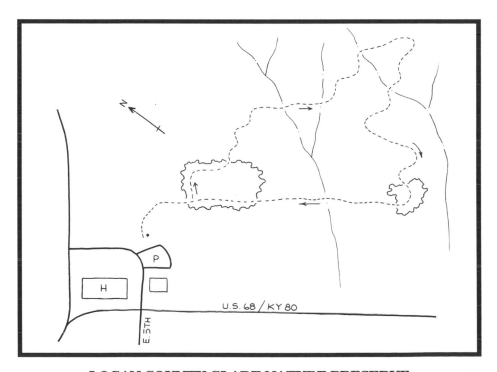

LOGAN COUNTY GLADE NATURE PRESERVE

63

VI. HIKING AREAS OF EAST-CENTRAL KENTUCKY

18. Cherokee Park

19. Beargrass State Nature Preserve

20. Taylorsville Lake State Park

21. Bernheim Arboretum & Research Forest

22. Buckley Wildlife Sanctuary

23. Raven Run Nature Sanctuary

24. Abraham Lincoln's Birthplace
    National Historic Site

25. Green River Lake State Park

26. Barren River Lake State Resort Park

27. Lake Cumberland State Resort Park

28. Dale Hollow Lake State Park

29. Laurel River Lake & Vicinity

30. Cumberland Falls State Resort Park

31. Natural Arch Scenic Area

32. Big South Fork National River
    & Recreation Area

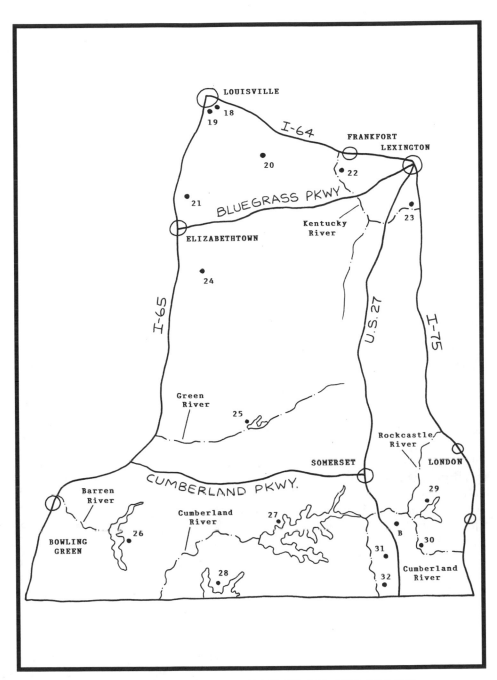

HIKING AREAS OF EAST-CENTRAL KENTUCKY

18 CHEROKEE PARK

Beargrass Creek Loop
Distance: 2.5 miles
Terrain: hilly
Walking time: 1.5-2.0 hrs.

Cherokee Park, in east-central Louisville, is bisected by the Middle Fork of Beargrass Creek. With its wooded hills and rolling meadows, this 409 acre refuge entices local residents and out-of-towners alike.

While most Park visitors head to the playgrounds, ball fields and picnic areas, a fine hiking trail will be found at the eastern end of the preserve. This 2.5 mile path, open to hikers and horsemen, makes an elongated loop along and across Beargrass Creek.

Directions: From I-64, take Exit #8, turn southwest on Grinstead Drive and then left (east) on Lexington Road (Alternate U.S. 60). Proceed to Alta Vista Road (approximately .75 mile) and turn right. Descend southward to the Park Road (about 1 mile), turn left and park in the lot just west of the bridge and north of the Creek (see map).

Route: From the parking lot, the **Beargrass Creek Loop** (our terminology) leads westward above the north bank of the stream. Within a short distance you will reach an old millstone (M); the trail forks here. Bear right, staying on the north side of the creek and angle up to the Park Road. Hike past some rock cliffs along the road and pick up the Trail once again, climbing into a hillside woodland. Buildings of the Presbyterian Theological Seminary will appear intermittently on your right before the trail descends back to the creek and crosses a gravel lane.

The path now leads through open woodlands and meadows of the **Nettleroth Bird Sanctuary (NB)** and soon reaches a trail intersection (see map). Turn right and then bear left at the next three forks, staying on the main path as it climbs the ridge and crosses Maple Road. A short excursion atop the hill is followed by a gradual descent to the Park Road.

Turn left along the road, cross the bridge and pick up the Trail on the south side of the intersection (see map). The return trip is a hilly journey along and atop the valley wall, dipping in and out of the rich deciduous forest. Two roads will be crossed before the trail descends to ford Beargrass Creek near the millstone (M). Return to the parking lot via your original entry path.

Entering the Nettleroth Bird Sanctuary

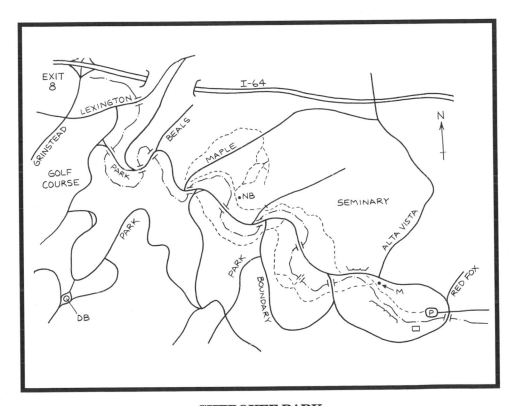

CHEROKEE PARK

19 BEARGRASS CREEK STATE NATURE PRESERVE

Combined Loop Hike
  Distance: 1.4 miles
  Terrain: hilly
  Walking time: 1 hour

Adjoining Joe Creason Park, in south-central Louisville, **Beargrass Creek State Nature Preserve** is a popular birdwatching and nature study area. This 41 acre refuge harbors over 180 species of plantlife and more than 150 species of birds have been identified within its boundaries. Dedicated in 1982, the Preserve also protects the site of a World War I Army Camp (Camp Zachary Taylor) which operated as an enlistment facility from 1917 to 1921.

Directions: From I-264 (the Watterson Expressway), 4 miles west of I-64, take Exit #15A (KY 1703) and head north on Newburg Road. Drive 1 mile and turn left on Trevilian Way. Proceed another .5 mile and turn right into Joe Creason Park, which is just north of the Louisville Zoo. Park in the lot next to the Metro Parks Office Building (MP).

Route: Several interconnecting trails run across a wooded hillside and along the course of Beargrass Creek. We suggest the following combined loop hike, which yields a distance of approximately 1.4 miles. At the time of our visit, in 1994, there were only a few "State Nature Preserve" signs at the trailheads; trail junction signs were absent.

From the parking lot at the Metro Parks Building (MP), descend eastward to a Park roadway (see map). Turn left and descend further along this narrow lane to the Beargrass Creek bridge. Just before the bridge, turn left and pick up a trail that follows the Old Prather Road, paralleling the Creek. Bypass the first two trails on your left and continue along the old road bed as it leads southwestward along the edge of a swamp forest.

Upon reaching a boardwalk intersection, turn left and ascend the wooded hillside via a winding route. Turn right at the next two trail junctions (see map) and begin a steep descent back to the old road bed. Turn left on the Old Prather Road, bypass a narrow path on your left, cross a wooden bridge and bear left at the trail junction; the trail to the right leads out to an apartment complex.

The main trail curves southward and begins a gradual ascent to Sheridan Avenue. Climb to the roadway, turn left and hike back to the Metro Parks Building (MP), passing the Nature Clubhouse (NC) and other Park facilities along the way.

A winter morning on Beargrass Creek

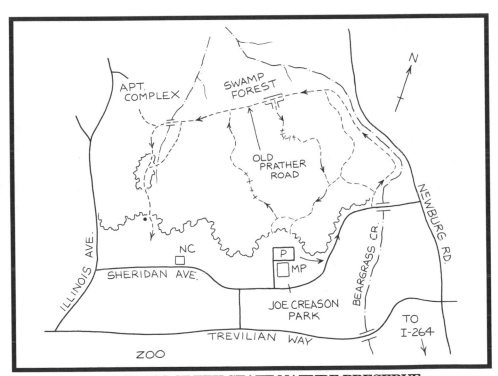

BEARGRASS CREEK STATE NATURE PRESERVE

Snyder Hollow Loop
  Distance: 2 miles
  Terrain: rolling, few hills
  Walking time: 1.5 hours

Beech Creek Loop A
  Distance: 2.7 miles
  Terrain: rolling, some hills
  Walking time: 2 hours

B.C.A.- Possum Ridge Loop
  Distance: 5.5 miles
  Terrain: hilly
  Walking time: 3.0-3.5 hours

L.Beech Cr.- Salt River Vista
  Distance: 6.5 miles
  Terrain: hilly
  Walking time: 4.5 hours

Taylorsville Lake is a 3000 acre flood-control reservoir on the Salt River, approximately 25 miles southeast of Louisville. A Kentucky **State Park** now covers Possum Ridge, overlooking the north shore of the Lake.

Hikers and naturalists will find a 17.3 mile network of trails which lead across the ridgetop and descend to the Beech Creek and Little Beech Creek inlets (see map). These wide paths are open to foot travel as well as horseback riding; bicycles and motorized vehicles are not permitted on the trails.

Directions: From KY 55 on the north side of Taylorsville, turn east on KY 44. Drive 5.1 miles and bear right on KY 248; another 1.9 miles brings you to the Park entrance, on your right. Proceed 1 mile and park in the lot on the south side of the road, just east of the Visitor Center (VC). There are currently no camping or lodging facilities at the State Park.

Routes: The wide trails at **Taylorsville Lake State Park** were not well marked at the time of our visit (July, 1994). Generic "trail" signs were located at the trailheads but there were no markers at trail intersections and many of the paths were overgrown. Close attention to the map in this guide is thus recommended. We suggest the following dayhikes:

Snyder Hollow Loop (SHL). This 2 mile loop begins and ends at the common trailhead approximately 50 yards east of the parking lot (see map). The trail cuts eastward, winding along a meadow near the forest margin. After turning back to the northwest, the path enters the woods and descends along a stream bed. Turn left at the trail intersection for a short climb back to the road.

Beech Creek Loop A (BCLA). Perhaps the best dayhike at the Park, this 2.7 mile route begins and ends at the parking lot. Hiking counterclockwise, follow the trail across the Park road and then angle to the northwest through a wooded meadow. After passing an old farm pond, the trail enters the forest, dipping across tributaries of Beech Creek. The path curves back to the south near the Beech Creek inlet, passes a second pond and returns to the Park road.

Beech Creek Loop A - Possum Ridge Loop (5.5 miles). Follow the east arm

Open woodlands on
Beech Creek Loop A

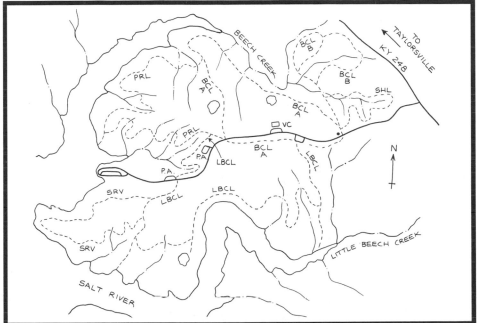

TAYLORSVILLE LAKE STATE PARK

of the **Beech Creek Loop A** to the Beech Creek inlet, as described above. After curving back to the south, watch for the **Possum Ridge Loop (PRL)**, on your right. This strenuous route undulates along the south wall of the inlet, crossing numerous drainages along the way. It eventually rejoins **Beech Creek Loop A** at the Park road (see map).

   Little Beech Creek (LBCL) - Salt River Vista Loop (6.5 miles). Adventurous hikers may want to tackle this double-loop route which heads southward from the parking lot and then turns westward above Little Beech Creek. Nearing the Salt River channel, the **Little Beech Creek Loop** cuts back to the north where it intersects the **Salt River Vista Loop**. The latter makes an elongated loop to the west and offer some fine views of Taylorsville Lake. Once back at the **Little Beech Creek Loop**, turn left and return to the Park road.

71

21 BERNHEIM ARBORETUM & RESEARCH FOREST

Tower Loop Trail
Distance: 1 mile
Terrain: rolling
Walking time: .75 hr.

Knob Top - D.C. Hollow - Iron Ore Hill
Distance: 4.5 miles
Terrain: hilly
Walking time: 2.5-3.0 hrs.

Jackson Hollow Trail
Distance: 1 mile
Terrain: hilly
Walking time: 1 hr.

Cull Hollow Trail
Distance: 1.5 miles
Terrain: hilly
Walking time: 1 hr.

Donated to the citizens of Kentucky by Isaac W. Bernheim, a German Jewish immigrant and founder of the I.W. Harper brand of whiskey, the **Bernheim Arboretum & Research Forest** covers 14,000 acres of restored farm land in the Outer Bluegrass Belt of the Lexington Peneplain. Two thousand acres comprise the nationally famous Arboretum which features over 1800 labeled species of plantlife, including the largest collection of American hollies in the U.S. A Nature Center (NC) houses educational exhibits which depict native flora and fauna of the southern Ohio Valley.

A fine network of hiking trails provides access to the Natural Forest Area, which blankets the ridge south and east of the Arboretum. Most trails originate along Tower Hill Road or on Paul's Point Loop (see map).

Directions: From I-65, take Exit 112 and head east on KY 245. Drive .8 mile to the entrance, on your right. The Arboretum & Research Forest are open weekends year round and on weekdays from March 15 to November 14. Admission is currently free on weekdays but an environmental impact fee is charged to non-members on weekends and holidays (currently $5.00 per vehicle).

The Isaac W. Bernheim Foundation, a private, nonprofit corporation, owns and manages the Arboretum & Research Forest. For information on becoming a "Friend of Bernheim," contact them at 502-955-8512. Membership fees support educational programs and maintenance of the plant collections, trails and estate facilities.

Routes: With the exception of the **Guerilla Hollow Loop (GHL)**, which was not researched for this guide, the hiking trails within Bernheim's Natural Forest all originate along **Tower Hill Road** or on **Paul's Point Loop**. These areas are reached by following Tower Hill Road southeast from the Nature Center (NC; see overview map). The gate to the Natural Forest Area is closed and locked 1/2 hour before the Arboretum closes (keep this in mind when planning your hike!).

A view from the Knob Top Trailhead

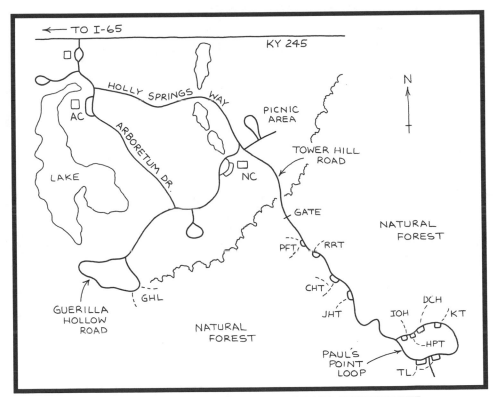

BERNHEIM ARBORETUM & RESEARCH FOREST
(OVERVIEW MAP)

TRAILS OFF TOWER HILL ROAD

The **Poplar Flat (PFT)** and **Rock Run Trails (RRT)** will be noted along Tower Hill Road, a short distance south of the gate; these trails are rather short and were not researched for this guide. Further along, however, are two trails that offer excellent dayhikes:

Cull Hollow Trail (CHT). This 1.5 mile loop begins at a parking area on the west side of Tower Hill Road, .9 miles south of the Forest gate. Cross the stream and hike the loop clockwise, climbing westward above a tributary. After dipping across several drainages, the trail loops to the north and then heads eastward atop the ridge. Two broad switchbacks bring you back down to the trailhead.

Jackson Hollow Trail (JHT). A shorter version (1 mile) of the Cull Hollow Trail, this path also originates along Tower Hill Road, 1.2 miles south of the gate. Hiking the loop clockwise, you will head upstream for a short distance, passing rock cliffs along the way. The trail then crosses the main creek and climbs to the northwest above a side stream. Once atop ridge, the path angles to the northeast and then begins a winding descent to the trailhead area.

TRAILS OFF PAUL'S POINT LOOP

Five trails originate along **Paul's Point Loop**, a one-way drive at the end of Tower Hill Road.

The **High Point Trail (HPT)** is a short excursion to the pinnacle of the ridge and the **Tower Loop (TL)** is a 1 mile (roundtrip) path to the site of the Forest's old firetower; the tower is fenced off and cannot be climbed by visitors.

Knob Top - D.C. Hollow - Iron Ore Hill Loop. The best dayhike within Bernheim's Natural Forest is achieved by combining sections of the **Knob Top (KT)**, **Double Cabin Hollow (DCH)** and **Iron Ore Hill (IOH) Trails**. This combined route yields a hike of 4.5 miles; due to the hilly terrain, this route is moderately strenuous and is recommended for fit and experienced hikers.

From the **Knob Top** parking lot you are treated to a fine view of forested hills to the northeast. Follow either arm of the **Knob Top Trail** and descend into the forest, soon intersecting the **Double Cabin Hollow Trail (DCH)**. Turn right and begin a long, winding descent to the valley floor, eventually turning westward along the primary stream.

Angling to the southwest, the **Double Cabin Hollow Trail** climbs along a major tributary and intersects the **Iron Ore Hill Trail (IOH)** near the crest of the ridge. Turn right at this junction for an elongated loop to the northwest. After curving back to the southeast, the trail negotiates several drainages enroute to Paul's Point Loop.

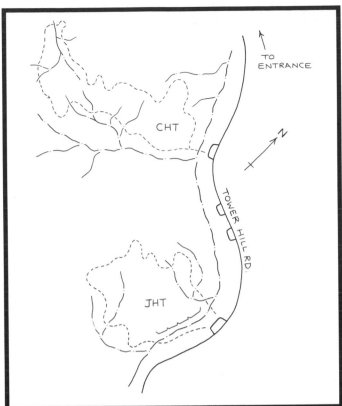

**CULL HOLLOW
TRAIL**

**JACKSON
HOLLOW TRAIL**

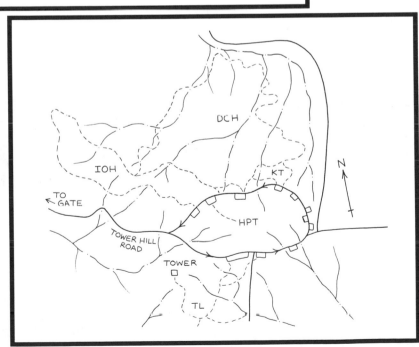

TRAILS OFF PAUL'S POINT LOOP

22 CLYDE E. BUCKLEY WILDLIFE SANCTUARY

Red Trail Loop
Distance: 2 miles
Terrain: rolling
Walking time: 1.5 hours

Blue Trail Loop
Distance: 1 mile
Terrain: rolling
Walking time: .75 hour

Combined Loop Hike
Distance: 3.5 miles
Terrain: rolling
Walking time: 2.5 hours

Donated to the National Audubon Society by Mrs. Emma Buckley as a memorial to her husband, the **Clyde E. Buckley Wildlife Sanctuary,** established in 1967, became the Society's first nature preserve in the Central U.S. The Sanctuary's 275 acres spread atop the east wall of the Kentucky River Valley and are accessed by a 3.25 mile network of hiking trails. A rich deciduous forest, wooded meadows and a marsh-rimmed pond characterize the preserve.

Directions: From I-64, just south of Frankfort, exit onto U.S. 60 and turn south. Proceed a short distance, turn right (west) on Route 1681 and drive 2.5 miles into Millville. Turn left on Route 1659, proceed 1.6 miles and turn right on Route 1964. After driving another .9 mile, continue straight ahead on Watts Ferry Road. Another .2 mile brings you to Germany Road; turn right and proceed 1.3 miles to the Sanctuary entrance, on your left.

The Sanctuary is open W-F, 9am-5pm, and Sat-Sun, 9am-6pm; it is closed Monday and Tuesday. A nominal fee is charged and is used to maintain the preserve. Plan to stop by the museum and display barn which house natural history exhibits.

Routes: Three hiking trails provide access to the Sanctuary; the **Red Trail (RT)** yields a hike of 2 miles while the **Blue Trail (BT)** covers a 1 mile loop. We suggest a combined, 3.5 mile route, which utilizes all three trails.

Pick up the **White Trail (WT)** at the southwest corner of the parking lot for a .25 mile excursion across the north wall of the Elk Lick valley and then angle to the west on the **Red Trail (RT)**. Cross a power line swath and bear left at the trail intersection, hiking westward and then northward through the forest; views of the Kentucky River Valley unfold during the "leafless months" of the year. Upon entering a wooded meadow, continue straight ahead along its western edge, bypassing cutoffs to the east.

After re-entering the forest, the **Red Trail** curves eastward, dips through a drainage and then cuts to the south just past a sinkhole (x). Follow the edge of the meadow to a multi-trail intersection and turn left; bear left again at the next fork, pass under the power lines and continue along this path as it curves the the south, skirts two sinkholes (x) and exits the woods near the display barn (D).

Winter at the old farm pond

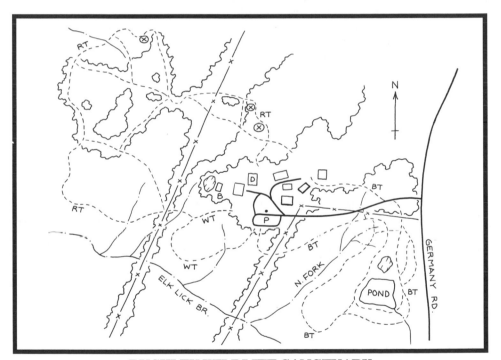

BUCKLEY WILDLIFE SANCTUARY

Cross through the parking lot and pick up the **Blue Trail (BT)** which enters the woods and curves to the east. Nearing the entry road the path forks; bear right above the north fork of Elk Lick (see map), soon angling to the east and circling an old farm pond. Continue along the **Blue Trail** as it leads north, crosses the entry road and ends near a cluster of barns.

23 RAVEN RUN NATURE SANCTUARY

Combined Loop Hike
  Distance: 3.2 miles
  Terrain: hilly
  Walking time: 2 hours

Dedicated to the protection of the natural and historic features of the Kentucky River Palisades region, **Raven Run Nature Sanctuary** is a superb destination for hikers. The 374-acre preserve, which stretches across the north wall of the Kentucky River Valley, harbors a wealth of flora and fauna, including over 300 species of wildflowers. Remnants of human habitation are found throughout the preserve, which is accessed by more than 7 miles of hiking trails; lettered markers are placed at trail intersections.

Directions: From I-75, just south of Lexington, take Exit 108 and head west on Man O War Blvd. Drive 2.5 miles and turn left (south) on Richmond Rd. Proceed 1.3 miles and bear right on U.S. 421 S; another 3.4 miles brings you to Route 1975 (Jacks Creek Pike). Turn right and drive 3.9 miles; Route 1975 splits off at this point; stay on Jacks Creek Pike for another 1.3 miles to the Sanctuary entrance, on your left.

The Sanctuary is open Wednesday through Sunday; hours vary with the season. Weekend crowds may limit access; call 606-272-6105 before your visit.

Route: Over seven miles of hiking trails provide access to the Sanctuary. We suggest the following 3.2 mile loop.

At the end of the service road, just north of the Nature Center (NC), turn right (east) on the **Red Woodland Trail (RWT)** , soon descending along a rock wall toward Chandler Creek. At intersection **A**, a side trail leads out to the remnants of a lime kiln (LK). Continue eastward on the **Red Woodland Trail** to an overlook above the Kentucky River; 100 feet above the River, you are treated to a spectacular view of rock cliffs (palisades) that line the gorge.

Hike to the northwest above the valley of Raven Run Creek, remaining on the **Red Woodland Trail** and bypassing side trails at intersections **D-L** (see map). At intersection **M**, descend to the former site of Evans Mill (circa 1820), which was one of many water-powered mills along this section of the Kentucky River.

Ascend back to the **Red Woodland Trail** and hike southward above the South Fork of Raven Run Creek, passing a spring (SP) along the way. At intersection **P**, turn left (east) on the north arm of the **Blue Woodland Trail (BWT)**, climbing through the forest to the preserve's central meadow. You will exit the woods near an old corn crib (CC) and the sanctuary's amphitheater (AT). Hike southward through the meadow, returning to the Nature Center (NC) and completing a 3.2 mile loop.

The Palisades Overlook

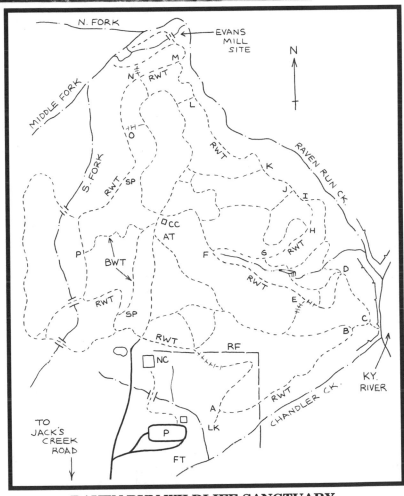

RAVEN RUN WILDLIFE SANCTUARY

24 ABRAHAM LINCOLN'S BIRTHPLACE NATIONAL HISTORIC SITE

Double Loop Hike
   Distance: 1.5 miles
   Terrain: rolling
   Walking time: 1 hour

Thomas and Nancy Lincoln, of Elizabethtown, Kentucky, moved to Sinking Springs Farm, near Hodgenville, in December, 1808. Their second child and our 16th President, Abraham, was born in the Lincoln's one room cabin two months later.

Abraham Lincoln's Birthplace was set aside as a national park in 1916 and was dedicated as a National Historic Site in 1959. While most of the visitors flock to the reconstructed cabin and other historic exhibits, hikers and naturalists will want to explore the fields and woodlands of the Lincoln's 19th Century Farm.

Directions: From I-65, take Exit 81 and head east on KY 84. Drive 8.6 miles to Hodgenville and turn right (south) on KY 61/U.S. 31E. The Historic Site will be 2.5 miles ahead.

Route: A 1.5 mile double-loop trail begins at a picnic area on the east side of KY61, a short distance northeast of the main entrance (see map). The northern loop is covered with fine gravel and wood chips, providing an even surface for walkers. Educational plaques, highlighting the natural and historic features of this woodland, are spaced clockwise along this loop.

The southern loop, which leads through an environmental study area, is an earthen path, devoid of the visitor accomodations described above. The eastern arm of this loop snakes through a rich, deciduous forest while the western arm skirts the edge of a meadow. Forest wildflowers are abundant here in April while their sun-loving cousins adorn the meadow from May through September.

The northern loop is a walker's delight

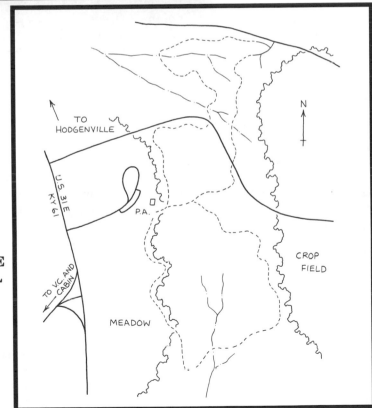

THE DOUBLE LOOP TRAIL

81

25 GREEN RIVER LAKE STATE PARK

Windy Ridge Trail
  Distance: 1.5 miles
  Terrain: hilly
  Walking time: 1 hour

Heading in Lincoln County, west of Mt. Vernon, the Green River drains a broad swath through central Kentucky as it flows westward to join the Ohio River near Evansville, Indiana. Green River Lake, an 8200 acre reservoir in the upper reaches of this vast watershed, is the site of a State Park that draws boaters, campers and fishermen to Taylor County.

Hiking at **Green River Lake State Park** is currently limited to the **Windy Ridge Trail**, a 1.5 mile excursion across a forested hillside, west of the Lake.

Directions: From the Cumberland Parkway, take Exit 49 and head north on KY 55. Drive 15 miles and turn right (southeast) on KY 1061. The Park entrance will be 1.4 miles ahead, on your left.

Route: The **Windy Ridge Trail (WRT)** begins at the northwest edge of the Miniature Golf area; park in the lot near the grocery store and campground entrance (see map).

Climb along the edge of the forest and enter the woods at the trail marker. The first section of the trail undulates through the forest, paralleling the Park road. Cross a power line swath and continue toward the northwest, eventually diverging from the roadway.

Bear right at the trail intersection, descending through open woodlands to the edge of Green River Lake. Bypass the return path and continue down to the shore, a nice secluded spot for a picnic lunch.

The return arm of the **Windy Ridge Trail** crosses several drainages and passes a fine viewpoint (V) before exiting the forest near the primitive campgrounds. Walk southward along the road and return to the parking lot.

Green River Lake from the Windy Ridge Trail

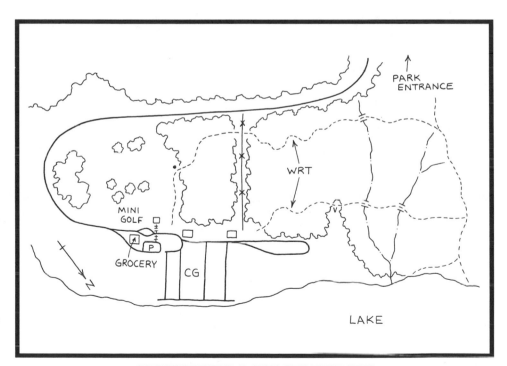

GREEN RIVER LAKE STATE PARK

Bike Trail
  Distance: 2.5 miles
  Terrain: rolling; paved
  Walking time: 1.5 hours

Lewis Hill Trail
  Distance: 1 mile
  Terrain: hilly
  Walking time: .75 hour

Lena M. Phillips Trail
  Distance: .75 mile
  Terrain: hilly
  Walking time: .5 hour

Renowned as a mecca for boaters and fishermen, **Barren River Lake State Resort Park** is also a popular destination for campers, golfers and naturalists. The Park covers over 2100 acres, stretching above the east shore of Barren River Lake. Access to its forested areas is provided by three hiking trails.

Directions: Take Exit 11 from the Cumberland Parkway and head south on U.S. 31E. Drive 11 miles to the Park entrance, on your right.

Routes: The **Bike Trail (BT)** is a 2.5 mile, paved loop, which begins and ends at the road intersection just east of the Lodge (L). The route crosses open fields, wooded meadows and tracts of hardwood forest. Along the way it skirts the Park's golf course which, while detracting from the woodland's serenity, has created a maze of natural habitats. Such areas, rich in "border zones" can be excellent for birdwatching.

The **Lewis Hill Trail (LHT)** is a 1 mile loop which also begins and ends at the road intersection just east of the Lodge (L). The trail's west arm descends to a creek bed and then climbs past a group of cabins (C) before turning eastward above the Park's beach area (see map). After curving to the north to ford a stream, the trail resumes its eastward journey, crossing numerous drainages along the way. Nearing the east end of its loop, the path climbs away from the lake basin and then turns northwestward to complete its 1 mile route.

The **Lena M. Phillips Trail (LMP)**, dedicated in March, 1980, honors the founder of the Kentucky Business & Professional Women's Association. This .75 mile path begins and ends near a picnic shelter east of U.S. 31E, .3 miles south of the Park's main entrance (see map). The trail loops through a mixed pine-hardwood forest, descending into a creek basin and then climbing back to the picnic area. Educational plaques are spaced along the route, introducing visitors to the natural and historical features of the area. The trail itself was constructed by the Young Adult Conservation Corps.

A summer day on Barren River's Bike Trail

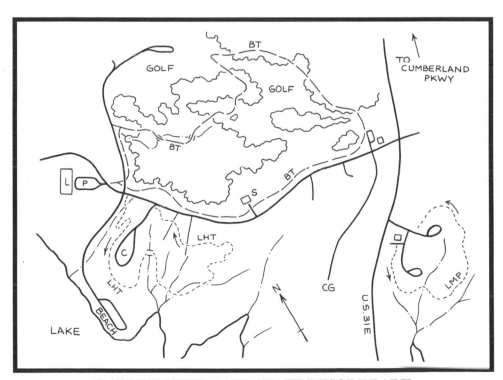

BARREN RIVER LAKE STATE RESORT PARK

27 LAKE CUMBERLAND STATE RESORT PARK

Lake Bluff Nature Trail
  Distance: 3.7 miles
  Terrain: hilly
  Walking time: 2.0-2.5 hrs.

Take Lake Powell of the American Southwest, douse it with 40 inches of annual precipitation for 20,000 years or so and you will have the picturesque setting of Lake Cumberland. Completed in 1952, this spectacular reservoir has over 1250 miles of shoreline and stretches for over 100 miles from east to west. The Lake's countless wooded coves entice houseboaters and fishermen throughout the year.

Lake Cumberland State Resort Park, the access point for many of these water lovers, sprawls for over 5 miles above the northwest shore of the Lake. White-tailed deer are common along the Park's roadways and Lodge residents have established the dubious tradition of enticing raccoons, skunks and woodchucks from the adjacent woods with after dinner handouts. Hikers will enjoy a fine, 3.7 mile nature trail, which circles the east end of the Park and offers some magnificent views along the way.

Directions: From Somerset, head west on the Cumberland Parkway to Russell Springs (the U.S. 127 Exit). Drive south on U.S. 127 and proceed approximately 14 miles to the Park entrance, on your left.

Route: Park at the Lodge and pick up the **Lake Bluff Nature Trail** next to the Nature Center (NC). The trail descends to cross a stream and then winds along an inlet of Lake Cumberland, fording numerous drainages. At the trail intersection, turn left, cross the primary inlet stream and ascend the lakeside ridge. Once atop the ridge, turn left and walk out to a spectacular overlook (V).

After taking in the view, hike southward atop the ridge where forest clearings offer additional overlooks. The trail eventually curves to the west and intersects the Cottage Road. Turn right and hike along the road, picking up the trail past the second driveway on your left (across from the boat storage area).

The **Lake Bluff Trail** continues westward through meadows and open woodlands, crossing the main Park road. Curving northward, it crosses another roadway and then loops to the east to ford an inlet stream. The trail now follows the rim of the basin as it parallels the shoreline and passes behind a group of cabins. After another stream crossing, the path climbs to Pumpkin Creek Lodge (PCL) which commands a fine view of the Lake.

From the Pumpkin Creek Lodge the **Lake Bluff Trail** curves eastward, crosses the State Dock Road and then angles toward the main Lodge where it ends at a wooden deck.

One of many fine views from the Lake Bluff Trail

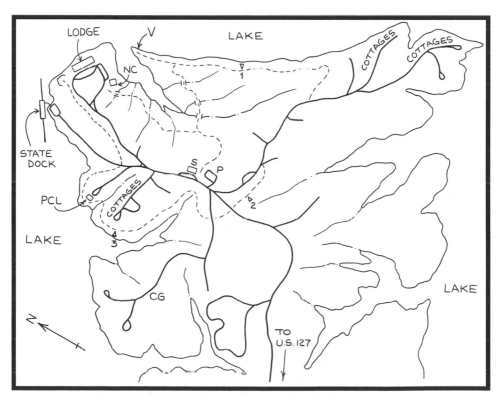

LAKE CUMBERLAND STATE RESORT PARK

28 DALE HOLLOW LAKE STATE PARK

Eagle Point Trail
Distance: 3.6 miles roundtrip
Terrain: rolling; few hills
Walking time: 2 hours

Charlie Groce Trail
Distance: 6.2 miles roundtrip
Terrain: rolling; hilly near lake
Walking time: 4.0-4.5 hours

Boom Ridge Trail
Distance: 8.2 miles roundtrip
Terrain: rolling; some hills
Walking time: 5.0-6.0 hours

Hoots Branch via Boom Ridge
Distance: 3.4 miles roundtrip
Terrain: rolling
Walking time: 2 hours

Renowned for its clear water, undeveloped shoreline and small-mouth bass production, **Dale Hollow Lake** was created by a dam on the Obey River in 1943. This 27,700 acre reservoir, which straddles the Kentucky-Tennessee border, is now home to **Dale Hollow Lake State Park**. The 3400 acre Park is draped across a series of wooded ridges, overlooking the north shore of the Lake. Access to remote sections of the Park is via a 13.4 mile network of jeep trails and old logging roads; closed to motorized vehicles, these wide paths are now reserved for hikers, horseback riders and mountain bikers.

Directions: From the junction of U.S. 127 and KY 90, head west on KY90. Drive almost 10 miles and turn south on KY 449. Follow this road for 4.5 miles to KY 1206. KY 1206 leads 3.5 miles to the State Park entrance.

Routes: The wide paths at **Dale Hollow Lake State Park** lead from the campground (CG) area to a number of points along or above the Lake. Those not using the campgrounds should park in a lot just west of the check-in gate.
We suggest the following dayhikes:
Eagle Point Trail (EPT). Perhaps the best dayhike at the Park, this 1.8 mile trail (3.6 miles roundtrip) leads southward from the campground, passes Cindy Cave (CC) and ends at Eagle Point (EP) which commands a spectacular view of the Lake; the view takes in islands and peninsulas that straddle the Kentucky-Tennessee line.
Charlie Groce Trail (CGT). This 3.1 mile trail (6.2 miles roundtrip) curves northward and then eastward from the campground entrance. After winding through meadows and open woodlands, the trail descends through forest to the Fanny Creek inlet of Dale Hollow Lake.
Boom Ridge Trail (BRT). Just over 4 miles in length, this is the longest trail in the Park and serves as access to numerous side trails. The trail begins at the campground entrance, crosses the main Park road and then heads SSW to the tip of Boom Ridge, in northern Tennessee. Branching from this central corridor are the **Hoots Branch Trail (HBT)**, the**Powerline Trail (PLT)**, the **Short Ridge Trail (SRT)**, the **Brushy Ridge Trail (BR)**, the **Wildcat Ridge Trail (WR)** and the **Groce Ridge Trail (GRT)**.

*Looking south
from Eagle Point*

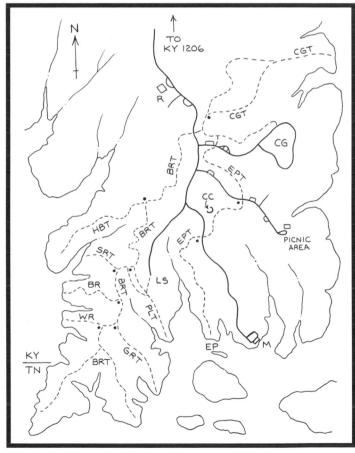

**DALE HOLLOW
LAKE
STATE PARK**

Hoots Branch Trail via Boom Ridge Trail. The **Hoots Branch Trail** is the longest (1.2 miles) spur trail from Boom Ridge. Its junction with the **Boom Ridge Trail** is approximately .5 mile SW of the campground entrance (see map); the roundtrip hike to the tip of Hoots Branch Ridge is thus 3.4 miles.

29 LAUREL RIVER LAKE & VICINITY

Distance: Dayhikes range from .5 to 10.7 miles
Terrain: hilly; some hikes cross rolling terrain
Walking time: Dayhikes of .5 to 5 hours

The Rockcastle, Laurel and Cumberland Rivers converge near the western edge of the Appalachian Plateau in southern Kentucky. These streams and their numerous tributaries have carved a vast network of ravines, "hollows" and rock-walled gorges through the Plateau, creating a scenic wonderland for outdoor adventurers.

Laurel River Lake, a flood-control and recreation reservoir on the Laurel River, is the centerpiece of this natural haven. Wooded peninsulas jut into the Lake, providing access for boaters, fishermen and other water sportsmen. Several of the hiking trails in this region run atop or along these ridges, yielding fine views of the reservoir.

We have grouped the hiking trails of the **Laurel River Lake Region** into three regions: **Trails North of the Lake**, **Trails West of the Lake**, and **Trails South & East of the Lake.** Each of these regions is subdivided into specific hiking areas.

Directions: To reach hiking areas north of Laurel River Lake, take Exit 38 from I-75 and head southwest on KY 192. From the Exit, road distances will be:

Bald Rock (BR): 14.5 miles   **Forest Road 774:** 15.6 miles
Forest Road 62: 16.9 miles   **KY 1193 junction:** 19 miles
Bee Rock Area (BE): 23 miles

To reach areas west of Laurel River Lake, take Exit 38 from I-75 and head southwest on KY 192. Drive 19 miles to KY 1193; from the KY 192/KY 1193 junction, head south on KY 1193. The turnoff to the **Rockcastle Recreation Area (RC via KY 3497)** will be .5 mile ahead. The **KY 1277 junction**, access to the **Sheltowee Trace Trail (STT)** and **Bark Camp Creek (BCC) Trail**, will be 6.4 miles ahead (see overview map).

To reach the **Grove (G) Recreation Area**, on the Lake's south shore, take Exit 25 from I-75 and head southwest on U.S. 25W. Drive 5.3 miles to KY 1193 and turn right (north). Proceed 2.8 miles and turn right on Forest Road 558 which leads to the Recreation Area.

To reach the **Flatwoods (FW) Day Use Area**, on the Lake's eastern shore, take Exit 29 from I-75 and proceed northwest on KY 312. Drive 2 miles and turn left (west) on Level Green Road. This road ends at Forest Road 758; turn left on Forest Road 758 and follow this route to the Day Use Area.

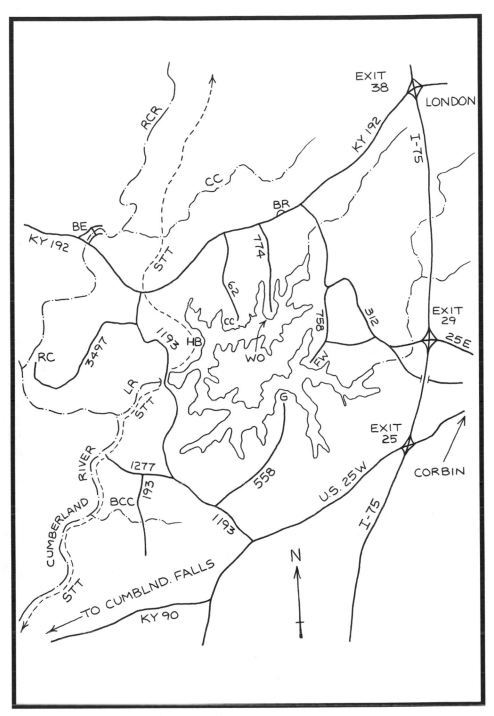

LAUREL RIVER LAKE & VICINITY

Bald Rock Picnic Area: This area, on the north side of KY 192, sits at the former site a a fire tower, atop the south wall of the Cane Creek Valley. Two trails are accessed from here:

Sugar Tree Hollow Trail (407). Almost 1.3 miles in length, this trail circles the Bald Rock Picnic Area, descending toward Cane Creek via one tributary and returning along a second stream. At the bottom of its loop, the trail intersects the **Cane Creek Trail**.

Cane Creek Trail (410). This path originates along **Trail 407** and follows Cane Creek northwestward for 2.1 miles, ending at Forest Road 121. The roundtrip distance from the Bald Rock Picnic Area to Forest Road 121 is 5.5 miles.

Van Hook Falls via the Sheltowee Trace Trail (STT). The Sheltowee Trace Trail (see Chapter II) crosses through the Laurel River Lake region, trending SSW to NNE. One of the better access points is at the junction of KY 192 and KY 1193.

To reach **Van Hook Falls** from this lot, cross KY 192 and hike northward on the **Sheltowee Trace Trail**, descending along the Pounder Branch (PB) of Cane Creek. Cross Cane Creek via a bridge and ascend along the Van Hook Branch (VHB) to the falls (less than .5 miles from the bridge). The roundtrip hike from KY 192 to the Falls is approximately 5.5 miles.

Bee Rock Recreation Area: Located at the junction of Cane Creek and the Rockcastle River, this popular camping area provides access to four trails:

Rockcastle Narrows East (401). This 3.8 mile trail (7.6 miles roundtrip) begins at the East Campgrounds and follows the Rockcastle River upstream, crossing Cane Creek along the way. After passing "the Narrows," of the Rockcastle, the trail angles to the northeast and climbs to Forest Road 119.

Winding Stair Gap Trail (402). This 1.2 mile path (2.4 miles roundtrip), leaves **Trail 401** just north of the Cane Creek crossing and climbs 350 feet to Forest Road 119.

Rockcastle Narrows West (503). This hike to the "Narrows" of the Rockcastle River begins at the north end of the West Campgrounds and follows the River for 1.3 miles (roundtrip distance: 2.6 miles). Forest Road 807 may be used to connect this route with **Trail 529** (see map).

Bee Rock Overlook Trail (529). This loop hike to Bee Rock, which towers 200 feet above the Rockcastle River, passes a number of rock formations and recessed caves. The entire loop, including a return walk along the campground road, covers 2.5 miles.

Cold Rock School Trail (430). Originating at a lot near the south end of Forest Road 774 (see maps on pages 91 & 95), this 3.3 mile trail uses series of earthen paths and gravel roads to reach the **White Oak Campground (WO)**

The Rockcastle River from the Bee Rock Overlook

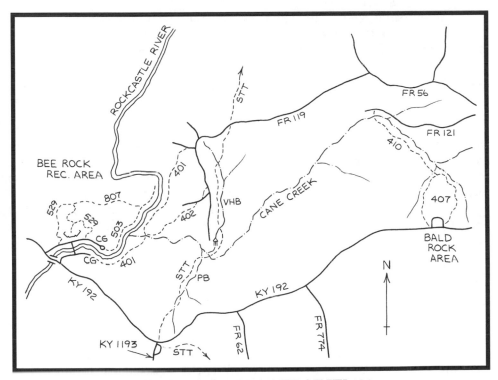

HIKING TRAILS NORTH OF KY 192
BALD ROCK - SHELTOWEE TRACE - BEE ROCK

on the north shore of Laurel River Lake; the campground can be reached by boat or foot travel only. The roundtrip hiking distance from Road 774 is 6.6 miles.

Craigs Creek Trail (420). The trailhead for this 2.2 mile route (4.4 miles roundtrip) is at the group campground off Forest Road 62 (see maps on pages 91 & 95). The trail winds southward to the Craigs Creek boat ramp, yielding views of the Lake along the way.

Sheltowee Trace Trail: Holly Bay Campground to Laurel River Dam. This section of the **Sheltowee Trace Trail (STT)** covers 4.2 miles (8.4 miles roundtrip). Park at the Holly Bay Campground off the east side of KY 1193 (check in with the gate attendant) and hike southward to the Dam. The route crosses numerous drainages and offers spectacular views of Laurel River Lake along the way (see map next page).

TRAILS SOUTH & EAST OF LAUREL RIVER LAKE

Grove Recreation Area. This campground and boat launch area covers the tip of a peninsula that juts into Laurel River Lake at the north end of Forest Road 558 (see map next page). Five hiking trails are located here:

    Duff Branch Trail (440). This .7 mile trail (1.4 miles roundtrip) leads from the C loop parking lot to two boat-in campgrounds on the south shore of Laurel River Lake. A fine ridgetop overlook is reached before descending to the lakeshore.

    Spruce Creek Overlook (441). Originating near the Loop B restrooms, this .3 mile loop leads out to an observation deck, descends toward the lakeshore and then climbs back along a stream bed.

    Fishing Point Trail (442). This 1.2 mile loop begins at the C loop parking lot and leads down to the south shore of Laurel River Lake.

    Singing Hills Trail (443). Beginning near the Grove Campground entrance, this .3 mile loop leads to an overlook that is famous for its sunset views across Laurel River Lake.

    Oak Branch Trail (444). This .4 mile trail (.8 miles roundtrip) leads from the A loop restroom to the boat launch area on the west side of the peninsula.

Flatwoods Trail (470). The Flatwoods Day Use Area, offering picnic grounds and a boat launch, is at the west end of Forest Road 758 on the east shore of Laurel River Lake. The **Flatwoods Trail** winds along the shoreline and yields a 2 mile loop hike (excluding the easternmost section which leads down to the boat launch).

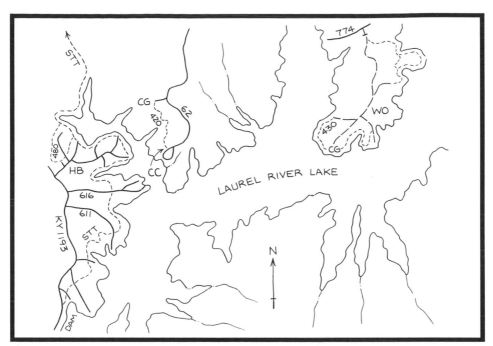

HIKING TRAILS ON THE NORTH SHORE

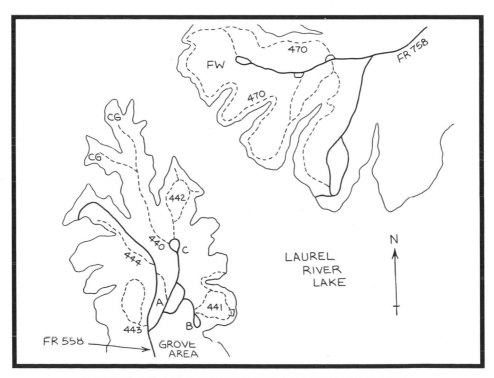

HIKING TRAILS SOUTH & EAST OF THE LAKE

Rockcastle Recreation Area: Located at the junction of the Rockcastle and Cumberland Rivers, this Recreation Area is 6 miles west of KY 1193 and is reached via KY 3497. There are 5 hiking trails at the Rockcastle Recreation Area; we have combined them into two loop hikes:

Dutch Branch-Scuttle Hole Overlook Trail (404). The **Dutch Branch** section of this trail begins along the campground access road and makes a .75 mile loop around the lower portion of Dutch Branch Creek (DB). In doing so, it passes beneath rock cliffs and ledges; a connector path leads up through "Scuttle Hole," a gap in the rock wall, joining the **Dutch Branch Trail** with the **Scuttle Hole Overlook Trail**. The latter leads out to a series of overlooks, 100 feet above the Rockcastle and Cumberland Rivers. The roundtrip hike to the overlooks (V) using both of these trails is 1.6 miles.

Ned Branch-Twin Branch-Lakeside Loop. A 7.5 mile loop hike can be achieved by combining three trails at Rockcastle Recreation Area. The **Ned Branch Trail (405)** leaves the north end of the campground and curves eastward, climbing along Ned Branch Creek (NB); this 1.9 mile trail ends at KY 3497. Cross the road and pick up the **Twin Branch Trail (406)** for a 1.1 mile descent to the east bank of the Cumberland River (actually the backwaters of Lake Cumberland). Head west on the **Lakeside South Trail (412)** which follows the shoreline back to the boat launch area. Hike northward on the roadway to your parking location.

Sheltowee Trace Trail: KY 1277 to Cumberland Falls. By using two cars (or by arranging transportation) one can plan a 10.7 mile dayhike on the **Sheltowee Trace Trail (STT)** from the mouth of the Laurel River (at the west end of KY 1277) to Cumberland Falls State Park. Hiking southward (upstream), you will travel along the east bank of the Cumberland River. Stream crossings at Bark Camp Creek (BCC) and Dog Slaughter Creek (see Cumberland Falls State Park map, page 99) may be impassable during periods of high water.

Bark Camp Trail (413). This 2.6 mile trail (5.2 miles roundtrip) begins on the west side of Forest Road 193, 2 miles south of KY 1277. The trail follows the Creek downstream to its junction with the Cumberland River, where the path intersects the **Sheltowee Trace Trail (STT)**. Rock cliffs, recessed caves and a series of waterfalls add to the scenic beauty of this streamside hike.

Laurel River Lake

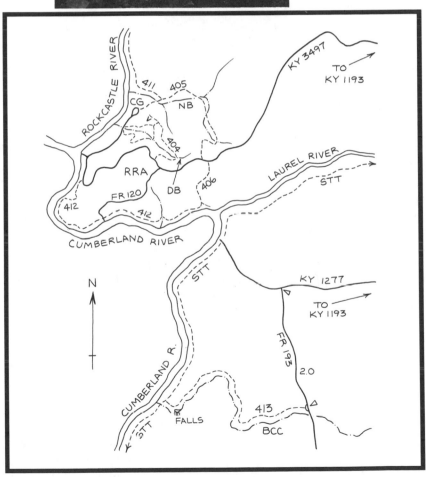

HIKING TRAILS WEST OF THE LAKE

30 CUMBERLAND FALLS STATE RESORT PARK

Sheltowee Trace-Trail 2 Loop
 Distance: 7.5 miles
 Terrain: hilly
 Walking time: 5 hours

Trail 11
 Distance: 5 miles roundtrip
 Terrain: hilly; steep areas
 Walking time: 3.0-3.5 hours

Combined loop (Trails 9 & 10)
 Distance: 3 miles
 Terrain: hilly; steep areas
 Walking time: 2 hours

Dog Slaughter Creek Trail
 Distance: 3.0 or 8.5 miles RT
 Terrain: rolling; few hills
 Walking time: 2 or 5.5 hours

Cumberland Falls, with a vertical drop of 68 feet and a width of 125 feet (at normal stage) is one of the most impressive cascades in America. Famous as the site of the only regularly occuring "moonbow" in the Western Hemisphere, the Falls is surrounded by **Cumberland Falls State Resort Park**, dedicated on August 21, 1930. The Park's rugged topography, rising above a bend in the Cumberland River, makes it an excellent destination for hikers.

Directions: From I-75 at Corbin, Kentucky, take Exit 25 and head southwest on U.S. 25W. Drive 8 miles and turn right (west) on KY 90. The State Park will be 7 miles ahead.

Routes: Sheltowee Trace-Trail 2 Loop. Known locally as the "Moonbow Trail," the **Sheltowee Trace Trail (STT)** enters the north side of the Park and follows the east bank of the Cumberland River to the KY 90 bridge; it then crosses to the west bank of the River (see map). **Trail 2** leaves the east end of a picnic area (northeast of the bridge) and follows the east bank of the Cumberland River for 2 miles to Bunches Creek (BC). It then turns northward, climbing along an old logging road to KY 90. North of the highway, **Trail 2** stays near the top of the ridge until it intersects a side trail to the old firetower (T); the tower is fenced off and closed to the public. Beyond the tower, the trail begins a gradual and then winding descent to the Cumberland River where it intersects the **Sheltowee Trace Trail**. By parking near the Falls (CF), the hiker can combine these two trails into a 7.5 mile loop.
 Trail 11. Those looking for some strenuous exercise can pick up **Trail 11** off **Trail 8**, across KY 90 from the campground entrance. **Trail 11** descends to cross a stream bed and then assaults the ridge via numerous switchbacks. Return from the ridgetop via the same route for a roundtrip hike of 5 miles.
 Combined Loop (Trails 9 & 10). This combined loop hike, totalling 3 miles, crosses through a State Nature Preserve and leads out to Eagle Falls (EF), a scenic cascade on the west bank of the Cumberland River. **Trail 9** begins on the north side of KY 90, west of the bridge (see map) and leads northward above the Cumberland River; views of Cumberland Falls

Cumberland Falls

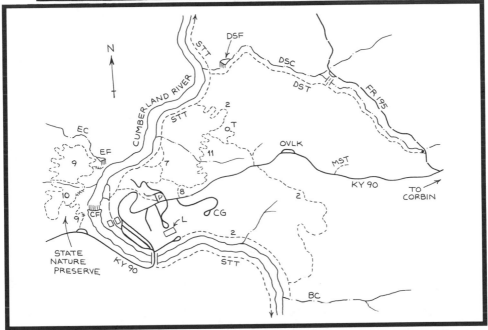

CUMBERLAND FALLS STATE RESORT PARK & VICINITY

unfold along the way. Bypass the cutoffs to **Trail 10** and proceed to a spur trail that drops steeply to the base of Eagle Falls. After taking in the sights, return to **Trail 9** which heads westward along Eagle Creek (EC) and then winds to the south, eventually intersecting **Trail 10**. Continue along the outside of the loop and then follow **Trail 9** back to the KY 90 trailhead.

Dog Slaughter Creek Trail (DST). This trail, outside the Park boundaries, is accessed off Forest Road 195 which cuts northwest from KY 90, east of the State Park (see map). Two trailheads service the trail, which follows Dog Slaughter Creek (DSC) westward to scenic Dog Slaughter Falls (DSF) and thence to the **Sheltowee Trace Trail**. The first trailhead, .9 miles north of KY 90 on FR 195, yields a roundtrip hike of 8.2 miles; the second trailhead, 2.9 miles north of KY 90, yields a roundtrip hike of 3 miles.

31 NATURAL ARCH SCENIC AREA

Natural Arch Trail
  Distance: 1.3 miles
  Terrain: hilly; stairs
  Walking time: 1.0-1.5 hours

Buffalo Canyon Trail
  Distance: 5.1 miles
  Terrain: rolling; few hills
  Walking time: 3.5 hours

Panoramic Trail
  Distance: 1 mile roundtrip
  Terrain: rolling
  Walking time: .75 hour

Gulf Bottom Trail
  Distance: 1.6 miles roundtrip
  Terrain: steep hill; stairway
  Walking time: 1.5 hours

Set aside as a National Scenic Area in 1961, this 945 acre preserve is characterized by rimrock cliffs, deep canyons and a spectacular sandstone arch. Relatively short, paved trails lead out to scenic overlooks while longer earthen paths take adventurous hikers to more remote sections of the park. Indeed, the **Natural Arch** and **Buffalo Canyon Trails** are the two most heavily utilized trails in the Somerset Ranger District.

Directions: From U.S. 27, 22 miles south of Somerset (and .5 mile south of the U.S. 90 east junction), turn west on KY 927. Proceed 1.7 miles to the Natural Arch lot or continue another 1.2 miles to the Great Gulf lot (G; see map).

Routes: Natural Arch Trail (510). Originating at the Natural Arch lot, this popular trail is paved all the way to the Natural Arch (NA). Enroute, the path loops eastward and then descends several sets of stairs. Upon reaching the valley floor, it intersects the **Buffalo Canyon Trail (508)** which leads westward toward Chimney Arch and the Great Gulf. Continue northward on the paved **Natural Arch Trail**, ascending gradually to the base of the sandstone arch. Hike up to the arch, which has a vertical clearance of 50 feet and a width of 90 feet. On the north side of the arch, the **Natural Arch Trail** continues as an earthen path which makes a .5 mile loop around the rock cliffs that extend westward from the arch. Complete the loop and return to the parking lot via your entry route.
  Buffalo Canyon Trail (508). This 5.1 mile loop cuts northward from the Natural Arch, following Spruce Creek downstream. Turn left (west) at the trail intersection on the bank of Cooper Creek and hike westward along this stream. The trail turns to the south at the Gulf Fork junction and heads upstream where it is intersected by the **Gulf Bottom Trail (509)**; bear left at this junction, following the **Buffalo Canyon Trail** as it parallels Cutoff Branch Creek and then winds eastward to meet the **Natural Arch Trail (510)**. Turn right and ascend back to the parking lot.
  Panoramic Trail (528). This .5 mile trail (1 mile roundtrip) begins at the Great Gulf lot (G) and leads northward atop a narrow ridge to two spectacular overlooks (see map).

The Natural Arch

**NATURAL
ARCH
SCENIC AREA**

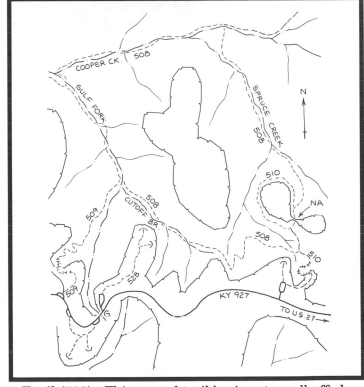

    Gulf Bottom Trail (509). This rugged trail begins at a pull-off along KY 927, .5 mile west of the Great Gulf lot. After making a broad curve to the east, the trail descends from the canyon rim via a steep metal stairway. Further switchbacks bring you to the valley floor where the **Gulf Bottom Trail** intersects the **Buffalo Canyon Trail** (see map). The roundtrip distance from KY 927 to this intersection is 1.6 miles.

32 BIG SOUTH FORK NATIONAL RIVER & RECREATION AREA

Distance: Dayhikes of 1.0 to 14.0 miles
Terrain: hilly; rolling terrain along River
Walking time: Dayhikes of 1.0   to 10 hrs.

Denuded by lumber companies and dotted with abandoned coal mines, western sections of the "Cumberland Plateau" were in desperate shape by the middle of the 20th Century. In an effort to restore the area's natural beauty and to inject much-needed funds into the regional economy, the U.S. Congress passed a bill to establish the **Big South Fork National River & Recreation Area** in 1974. The U.S. Army Corps of Engineers was enlisted to oversee land acquisition along the Big South Fork of the Cumberland River and to supervise development of recreational facilities.

The Recreation Area, managed by the National Park Service, now covers over 105,000 acres in Tennessee and Kentucky. Its forested hills are accessed by over 200 miles of hiking trails, including the southernmost portion of the **Sheltowee Trace Trail** (see Chapter II). Camping, rafting, kayaking, canoeing, fishing and horseback riding are also popular activities along the Big South Fork.

Directions: All areas within or near the Kentucky portion of the **Big South Fork National Recreation Area** are easily reached from Whitley City on U.S. 27 (see overview map).

To reach the **Yahoo Falls/Alum Ford Area**, head north on U.S. 27 for 1 mile and turn west on KY 700. The access road to Yahoo Falls (Road 660) will be 3.9 miles ahead and Alum Ford, on the River, will be 5.4 miles.

The **Laurel Creek Trail** (LRT, east of the Recreation Area) is reached by driving east on KY 478 from U.S. 27; its northeast trailhead will be 4 miles ahead, on your right. The southwest trailhead is accessed by heading south on U.S. 27 to East Appletree Road (E.AR; see overview map); turn east and drive 2.1 miles to the trailhead parking area, on your right.

The **Lick Creek Trail** (LCT, east of the Recreation Area) is west of Whitley City. Head south on U.S. 27 and turn west on KY 92. Drive into Stearns (S) and turn right (north) on KY 1651. The trailhead will be on a gravel lane, 1.5 miles north of Stearns, on your left.

The **Yamacraw Bridge Trailhead** is on the north side of KY 92, at the east end of the bridge, 5.1 miles west of U.S. 27.

To reach the **Blue Heron Area**, head south on KY 1651 from Stearns (S). Drive 1.1 mile and turn right (west) on KY 742; the campgrounds, overlook area and visitor center will be approximately 5 miles ahead.

Peters Mountain Trailhead (PM) is reached by heading southwest on KY 1363 from KY 92 at the west end of the Yamacraw Bridge. Drive 8.7 miles and turn left on a gravel road that passes the Bell Farm Horse Camp and then climbs another 4 miles to the summit of Peters Mountain ridge.

The Yamacraw Bridge on the Big South Fork

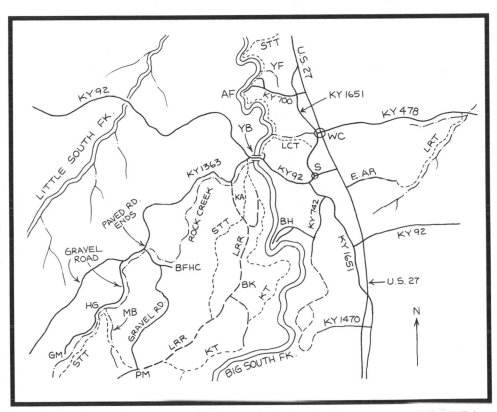

**THE BIG SOUTH FORK NATIONAL RIVER & RECREATION AREA
(KENTUCKY SECTION)**

Routes: This guide covers the Kentucky portion of the **Big South Fork National Recreation Area**. There are numerous potential dayhikes within and near this scenic preserve and we have divided our recommendations into two regions: **Trails north of KY 92** and **Trails south of KY 92**.

TRAILS NORTH OF KY 92

Yahoo Falls/Alum Ford Area. This popular hiking area is at the northern tip of the Recreation Area (see directions and map). We suggest the following dayhikes.

Yahoo Falls (YF). The **Yahoo Creek Trail (YCT)** leaves the north end of the parking area and curves to the east above rock bluffs. Within a short distance, the **Yahoo Falls Trail (YFT)** drops to the floor of the gorge via a long (and steep) metal stairway and then leads eastward to the base of the Falls. Those preferring to view the Falls from above should stay on the **Yahoo Creek Trail**. The roundtrip hike from the lot to the falls is approximately 1 mile.

Yahoo Arch (YA). This sandstone arch can be reached by following the **Yahoo Creek Trail** eastward from the Falls for another 1.2 miles; roundtrip hiking distance from the parking lot is 3 miles. Alternatively, the **Arch** can be accessed by hiking northward on the **Yahoo Creek Trail** from KY 700; the arch is 1.1 miles north of the road (2.2 miles roundtrip).

Yahoo Creek-Negro Creek-Alum Ford Loop. A 9.5 mile loop hike can be achieved by combining three trails, starting at the Yahoo Falls lot. Hike eastward on the **Yahoo Creek Trail (YCT)** passing above the Falls and continue southeastward toward Yahoo Arch and KY 700. Cross the road and pick up the **Negro Creek Trail (NCT; FR 6003)** which descends along Negro Creek for 2.3 miles, intersecting the **Sheltowee Trace Trail (STT)** on the east bank of the Big South Fork. Turn right (north) along the **Sheltowee Trace Trail**, cross through **Alum Ford** and continue back to the Yahoo Falls Area.

YAHOO CR.
NEGRO CR.
ALUM FORD
LOOP

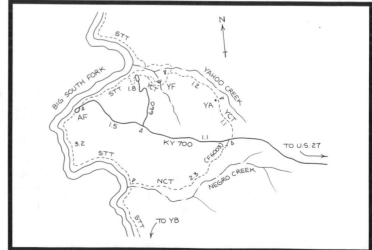

104

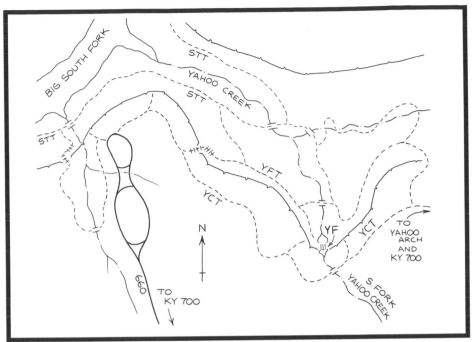

YAHOO FALLS AREA

Yahoo Falls

105

Laurel Creek Trail (LRT). Access to this scenic, stream side trail is via trailheads on either end, as described in the Directions for this chapter. The trail, which winds past rock ledges, small waterfalls and rhododendron thickets, is 4.1 miles long (8.2 miles roundtrip). Those planning a round-trip hike may want to park at the east trailhead, on KY 478, since the return route will be mostly downhill (see overview map, page 103).

Lick Creek Trail (LCT). This 4.4 mile trail (8.8 miles roundtrip) begins off the west side of KY 1651, 1.5 miles north of Stearns (S). After climbing across a ridge, the trail descends toward the Big South Fork along Lick Creek. Just short of its intersection with the **Sheltowee Trace Trail (STT)**, on the east bank of the River, the **Lick Creek Trail** skirts **Princess Falls**, a small but scenic cascade (see overview map, page 103).

Sheltowee Trace Trail (STT). The southernmost section of this 257-mile trail (see Chapter II) runs through and near the Big South Fork National Recreation Area; its route is illustrated on the overview map, on page 103. After entering the northern tip of the Recreation Area, the **Sheltowee Trace Trail** winds along the east bank of the Big South Fork, passing the Yahoo Falls Area, Alum Ford and Princess Falls. It crosses the Yamacraw Bridge (YB) and heads southwestward along the ridge that separates the Rock Creek and Big South Fork watersheds. Exiting the Commonwealth of Kentucky, the Trail ends in Tennessee's Pickett State Rustic Park.

 The section of the **Sheltowee Trace Trail** north of KY 92 is easily accessed at the Yamacraw Bridge Trailhead (see directions and overview map). Potential dayhikes along the Trail from this parking lot include:

 Yamacraw Bridge to Princess Falls on Lick Creek: 2 miles round-trip; an easy, 1.5 hour walk.

 Yamacraw Bridge to Alum Ford: 13 miles roundtrip; using two cars, this route becomes a moderate 6.5 mile hike in either direction. Plan at least 8 hours for the roundtrip hike.

 Yamacraw Bridge to Yahoo Falls Area: A one-way hike of 8 miles; the roundtrip distance (16 miles) is a bit long for a dayhike. Plan about 5 hours for the one-way trip.

TRAILS SOUTH OF KY 92

Blue Heron Area. Located in a bend of the Big South Fork, the **Blue Heron Area** occupies the site of an abandoned coal mining operation. This historic place can be accessed by KY 742, as described in the Directions, or by taking the **Big South Fork Scenic Railway**, from Stearns. The Blue Heron Visitor Center (VC) houses displays and artifacts from the glory days of coal mining along the Big South Fork.

106

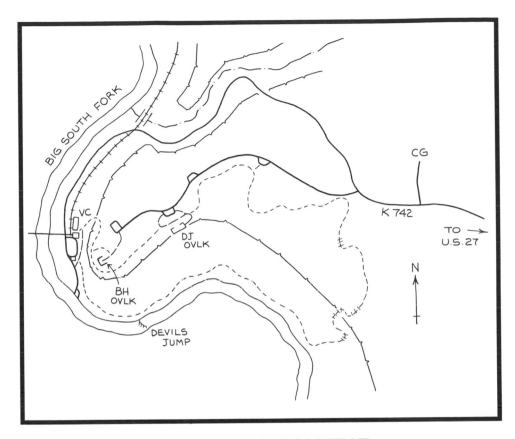

THE BLUE HERON LOOP TRAIL

Blue Heron Loop Trail. Hikers will be most interested in a 6.5 mile loop trail that offers scenic overlooks, riverside vistas and rugged topography. This loop trail is best accessed from any of the parking areas along the road that services the Blue Heron (BH) and Devils Jump (DJ) overlooks (see map on this page). Both Overlooks are reached by paved trails from their respective parking lots and both offer magnificent views of the Big South Fork Valley.

The loop trail passes beneath the Blue Heron Overlook, curves to the north and then descends to the valley floor, exiting the forest near the Blue Heron Visitor Center (VC). Hike southward along the paved lane and pick up the earthen path once again, heading east along the bank of the Big South Fork. Devils Jump, a Class IV rapid, will soon be encountered, a real challenge for the kayak crowd.

After leading along the River for almost 2 miles, the trail angles to the left and climbs the ridge via a series of stairs and switchbacks. Nearing the roadway, the path curves westward and heads back to the overlooks.

Sheltowee Trace Trail. South of KY 92, the **Sheltowee Trace Trail** begins a gradual climb to the crest of Laurel Ridge where it intersects the Laurel Ridge Road (LRR) for a second time (see overview map). It then follows this uneven, jeep road for almost 5.5 miles to Peters Mountain Trailhead (PM) where it turns northwest and descends to Rock Creek along Mark Branch (MB). Upon reaching the east bank of Rock Creek, the Trail turns southwest and follows the Creek upstream, into Tennessee. Potential day-hikes along this stretch of the **Sheltowee Trace Trail** include:

Yamacraw Bridge to Koger Arch (KA). Park at the trailhead on the east side of the Bridge, cross the Bridge and pick up the Sheltowee Trace just south of KY 92 (see map). A 3.5 mile hike takes you across Rock Creek, along its Grassy Fork and up to a side trail that leads to Koger Arch. Return to the Bridge via the same route, completing a roundtrip hike of 7 miles.

Yamacraw Bridge to Peters Mountain Trailhead. This long, strenuous dayhike covers 14 miles (one way). Plan to start at Peters Mountain (PM) in order to maximize your downhill mileage.

Mark Branch. This scenic, 2.3 mile section of the **Sheltowee Trace Trail** descends from Peters Mountain Trailhead (PM) to the east bank of Rock Creek (roundtrip distance 4.6 miles). One mile from the top, the trail passes a beautiful waterfall.

Kentucky Trail. This 27 mile trail, blazed with a red arrow, leads from the Peters Mountain Trailhead to the Yamacraw Bridge. Taking a less direct route than the Sheltowee Trace, it descends from the south side of Laurel Ridge Road and then winds northward along the west wall of the Big South Fork Valley. While this can be an excellent route for backpackers, the Trail and its access points are a bit remote for dayhikes.

The Big South Fork Valley

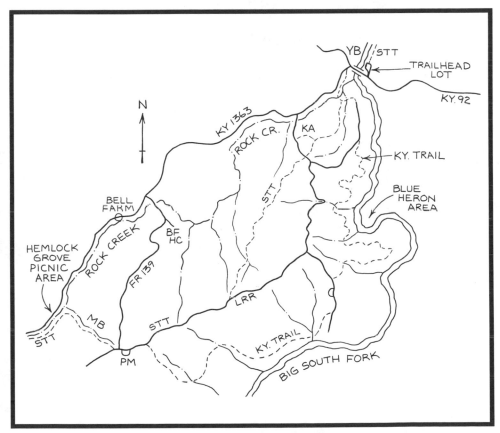

**THE SHELTOWEE TRACE & KENTUCKY TRAILS
(SOUTH OF KY 92)**

VII. HIKING AREAS OF NORTHERN KENTUCKY

33. Boone County Cliffs State Nature Preserve
34. Highland Cemetery Forest Preserve
35. Ft. Thomas Landmark Tree Trail
36. Doe Run Lake
37. Big Bone Lick State Park
38. Kincaid Lake State Park
39. Mullins Wildlife Management Area
40. Quiet Trails State Nature Preserve
41. Kleber Wildlife Management Area
42. Blue Licks Battlefield State Park
43. Carter Caves State Resort Park
44. Greenbo Lake State Resort Park
45. Jesse Stuart State Nature Preserve

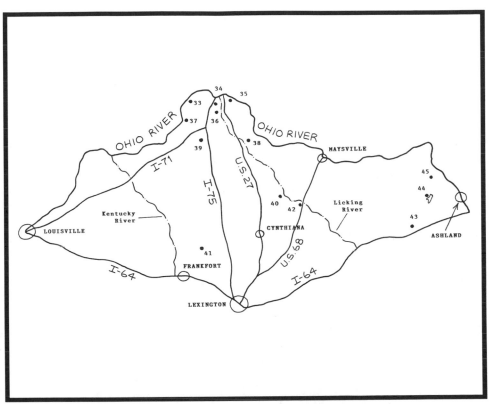

HIKING AREAS OF NORTHERN KENTUCKY

33 BOONE COUNTY CLIFFS
STATE NATURE PRESERVE

Main Trail Loop
   Distance: 2 miles
   Terrain: hilly
   Walking Time: 1.5 hours

East Boundary Loop
   Distance: 1 mile
   Terrain: hilly
   Walking Time: 1 hour

The Kansan Glacier plowed deep into western Ohio and eastern Indiana 1.2 million years ago. Outwash from the glacier spread sand, gravel and other till sediments across northern Kentucky and southern Indiana which have since hardened into sheets of "conglomerate rock." Subsequent erosion along the Ohio Valley has exposed outcrops of this conglomerate, forming impressive cliffs that rise above stream channels.

One of the best places to see these conglomerate cliffs is at **Boone County Cliffs State Nature Preserve**, west of Burlington. This 75 acre refuge, cloaked with old growth forest and carved by spring-fed streams, was brought under the protection of the Kentucky State Nature Preserve Commission through the efforts of the Kentucky Chapter of the Nature Conservancy. Access to the preserve is provided by two trail loops, described below.

Directions: From I-75 in northern Kentucky, take the Florence/Burlington Exit (Exit#181) and head west on Kentucky 18. Drive 10.3 miles and turn left on a small road that crosses a bridge, marked by a sign "Kentucky Nature Conservancy, 1.9 miles." This turnoff is approximately 6 miles west of Burlington. Follow this small road for 2 miles to a graveled lot, on your left. The Preserve is open dawn to dusk.

Routes: The **Main Trail Loop (MT)** begins next to the visitor registration box, makes a curve to the west and then climbs along the east wall of the Preserve's central gorge. After negotiating the first outcropping of Kansan conglomerate, the path winds eastward above a tributary where the **East Boundary Trail (EBT)** cuts off to the right (see map).

Continue along the **Main Trail** which begins a long excursion above the upper reaches of the central gorge, crossing numerous drainages. Curving back to the southwest, the trail runs atop a narrow ridge where deep ravines cut to either side. After a sharp bend to the east, watch for the **Ridge Loop Trail (RLT)**; bear left onto this short loop which leads out to the conglomerate cliffs and offers a broad view across the central gorge.

Continue along the **Ridge Loop Trail**, soon rejoining the **Main Trail** which leads southward across a forested ridge. Curving to the east, the trail descends to the creek and follows it downstream to a crossing near the road. Return to the lot along the roadway.

East Boundary Loop. The **East Boundary Trail (EBT)** leaves the east end of the parking lot, parallels the road and then turns northward, ascending

*Cliffs of Kansan
conglomerate line the
central gorge*

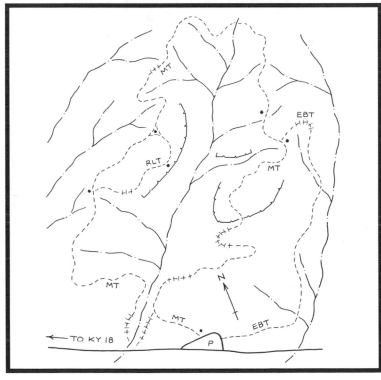

**BOONE
COUNTY
CLIFFS**

through a valley. After crossing a major tributary, the trail climbs along this stream and curves above its upper reaches on a long stairway. Upon reaching the intersection with the **Main Trail**, bear left and descend to the parking lot.

34 HIGHLAND CEMETERY FOREST PRESERVE

Combined Loop Hike (Trails1,2&3)
   Distance: 2.75 miles
   Terrain: hilly
   Walking time: 1.5 hours

Enamored with the natural beauty of **Highland Cemetery**, Gayle Pille approached the Superintendent with her idea of placing bluebird boxes on the Cemetery's open meadows. To her delight, the Cemetery Board was receptive to her project and informed her of their plans to enhance wildlife habitat throughout the Cemetery as a gift to the local community. Indeed, Gayle was enlisted to create a trail system for Highland Cemetery's forest preserve.

A member of the Kenton County Conservation Board and the Kentucky Trail Advisory Committee, Ms. Pille organized a group of volunteers who designed and constructed the current trail network from 1990-1991. The trails meander through a rich, hardwood forest that cloaks the eastern edge of the Cemetery. Wildflower gardens and wildlife food plots have also been developed on the grounds.

Highland Cemetery, the second largest cemetery in Kentucky, was formally dedicated on June 22, 1869. Covering 300 acres and having registered over forty thousand burials, the Cemetery occupies the site of a Civil War ammunitions depot. Thirteen Civil War soldiers, including Confederate General James Morrison Hawes, are buried at the Cemetery and trail construction volunteers unearthed a Civil War cannonball in the forest preserve.

Directions: From I-75 in northern Kentucky, take Exit #188A. Highland Cemetery is just southeast of the Interstate on the east side of Dixie Highway (U.S.127). Enter the main gate, pass the Cemetery office and continue to bear right at the intersections, eventually passing a lake. Park along the Cemetery drive near Lucerne Avenue (see map).

Route: Three trails provide access to Highland Cemetery's forest preserve. We suggest the following **combined loop** which yields a hike of approximately 2.75 miles.

Pick up **Trail 1** at the forest edge and descend into the woods along the Cemetery boundary. **Trail 1**, blazed with orange paint, soon angles to the left and roller coasters along the west wall of a deep ravine. Crossing numerous tributaries, the route eventually forks; bear right onto **Trail 2**, blazed with red paint, which descends toward the creek. Near the bottom of the slope, the remnants of an old well (w) sit along the trail.

As is too often the case in urban areas, new "development" is encroaching on this forest preserve. Just across the valley, a modern, 4-lane highway has cut a swath through the long undisturbed woods. **Trail 2** turns to the NW

*The trails provide access to
a rich hardwood forest*

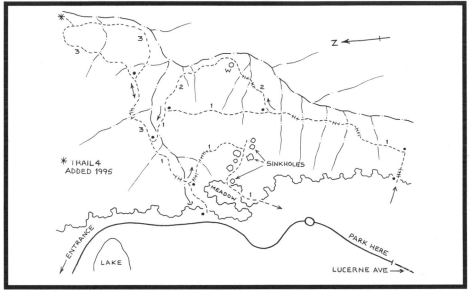

HIGHLAND CEMETERY FOREST PRESERVE

climbing above a major tributary and soon intersects **Trail 1**. Proceed straight ahead on **Trail 1** and begin a slow descent to a stream crossing.

On the opposite side of the creek is the cutoff to **Trail 3**. Turn right and follow this trail which is blazed with blue paint. After crossing a drainage, the trail forks. Take either route and complete a .4 mile loop, passing near the main creek at your lowest point. Return to **Trail 1** and continue upstream; just after crossing the main tributary the path forks. The right fork follows the stream and climbs directly to the Cemetery Road.

Take the left fork which ascends a stairway, dips across another ravine and then climbs to an area with numerous sinkholes. Turn right at the intersection, passing more sinkholes and a wooded meadow on your way to the Cemetery Road.

115

35 FORT THOMAS LANDMARK TREE TRAIL

Distance: 1.1 miles
Terrain: hilly
Walking time: 1 hour

Under the leadership of Bill Thomas, the Fort Thomas Tree Commission has taken steps to protect the city's most secluded parcel of old growth forest. Equipped with donated supplies and an army of volunteers, Thomas supervised construction of the **Landmark Tree Trail** during the winter and spring of 1993.

The 1.1 mile trail winds across a forested slope of the Ohio River Valley, dropping up to 200 feet from the trailhead on Carmel Manor Drive. Access to this secluded woodland was granted by the Carmel Manor Nursing Home and by Mr. Ed Wilbers; the city has leased the trail right-of-way from these private land owners and visitors should respect the arrangement by staying on the trail at all times.

A trail guide, available at the trailhead, describes 15 numbered trees that will be encountered along the route. Fourteen of these trees are at least 125 years old. These giants are immersed in a rich deciduous forest, dominated by maple, beech and buckeye trees. Colorful redbuds and numerous wildflowers adorn the forest in spring and birdwatching can be excellent along the winding trail.

Directions: From I-471, take the Grand Ave./Ky 1892 Exit (Exit #3) and turn east, winding up the Fort Thomas ridge. Drive 1.7 miles and turn right on S. Fort Thomas Ave. Pass Tower Park and turn left on Carmel Manor Drive. Park at the running track or near the trailhead which is just behind the U.S. Army Reserve Center; **do not** park at the Carmel Manor Nursing Home. The trail is for hikers only; bikes are not permitted.

Route: The **Landmark Tree Trail** begins on the southeast side of Carmel Manor Drive and enters the forest, merging with a path from the Nursing Home driveway. The trail forks at **Tree #1**, a 40 year old Kentucky Coffeetree; though not as old as the forest giants, this specimen is featured since it is the State Tree of Kentucky. Continue straight ahead to **Trees 2 & 3**, old Shumard Oaks. Across from Tree #3 a side path leads out to ruins from the old Ft. Thomas military depot.

Return to the main trail, descending past **Tree #4**, a 175 year old Northern Red Oak, and cross a stream. The trail now climbs on to **"Riverview Ridge,"** which yields a broad view of the Ohio River Valley during the "leafless" months of the year. **Tree #5**, another Northern Red Oak, stands near the crest of the ridge. Curving northward, the trail descends toward its lowest point. **Tree #6**, a 225 year old Sycamore with a 14 ft. circumference, is the largest tree in the preserve. The oldest (350 years) is **Tree #7**, a Chinkapin Oak. At **Tree #8**, a 140 year old White Ash, the trail curves back to

A sunny day on Riverview Ridge

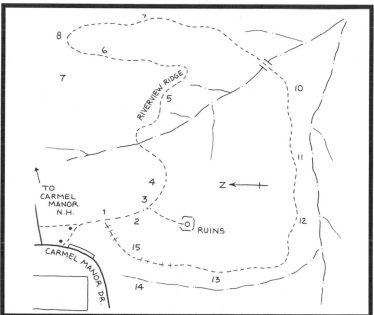

THE LANDMARK TREE TRAIL

the south where **Tree #9**, an old Northern Red Oak, has been used as a nest site by red-tailed hawks. The Trail recrosses the creek via a fine wooden bridge and curves westward, climbing along another stream. **Tree #10** is a 200 year old Northern Red Oak while **Trees 11-14** are all Shumard Oaks.

Leaving the main creek, the trail turns northward for a steep ascent along a tributary. **Tree #15**, a 175 year old Chinkapin Oak, signals to end of your loop hike; turn left on the entry trail to exit the forest. Please return your trail guide before leaving the preserve.

117

36 DOE RUN LAKE

North Shore Trail
  Distance: 2.2 miles roundtrip
  Terrain: rolling
  Walking time: 1.5 hours

Loop Trail
  Distance: .5 mile
  Terrain: hilly
  Walking Time: .5 hour

Sometimes the best hikes are found at the least known places. Such is the case at **Doe Run Lake**, a hidden jewel in Kenton County. Used primarily by local fisherman, the lake and surrounding forest offer a peaceful retreat near the rapidly developing suburbs of Northern Kentucky.

Directions: From the southern portion of I-275, east of I-75, take the Covington/Independence Exit (Exit #80) and head south on Kentucky 17 (Madison Pike). Drive 2.5 miles and turn right to "Old Ky 17," cross the creek and bear left on to Bullock Pen Road (marked by a Doe Run Lake sign). This road passes under a railroad trestle and leads to Doe Run Lake; park in the lot at the south end of the dam.

Routes: The **North Shore Trail (NST; our terminology)** begins at the north end of the dam where a path from the parking lot meets a short trail that descends from the entry road. This wide, graveled path leads westward above the north shore of Doe Run Lake, crossing stream beds along the way. Views of the Lake, more expansive in winter, are spaced along the route.

After hiking approximately 1 mile you will reach a clearing near the Bullock Pen Creek inlet, where numerous side trails lead down to the lake and creek. The main trail continues upstream, cutting across a sunny meadow and soon descending to **Bullock Pen Creek**. This is an excellent destination for a picnic lunch; a low waterfall, just downstream from the crossing, adds to the serenity and children will enjoy wading in the shallows. Fossil hunters will find plenty of bryozoans and brachiopods in the Ordovician rocks that line stream. Those who return to the lot from this creekside retreat will achieve a day hike of 2.2 miles.

If you're up for additional exercise, throw in the **Loop Trail (LT)**, a half mile excursion across the wooded ridge south of Bullock Pen Creek. Cross the stream, angle to the right and then bear left on a trail that climbs steeply through the forest. Leveling out atop the ridge, this trail eventually leads to a field; though the path enters the field, this is private land and we recommend backtracking to the **Loop Trail** (see map).

The western portion of the **Loop Trail** descends very steeply to Bullock Pen Creek where it intersects a streamside path. Turn right and follow this trail back to the **North Shore Trail**. Along the way you will cross and recross the creek; bypass a cutoff on your left just before the second stream crossing (see map). Return to the parking lot via the **North Shore Trail**, completing a total hike of 2.7 miles.

The North Shore Trail

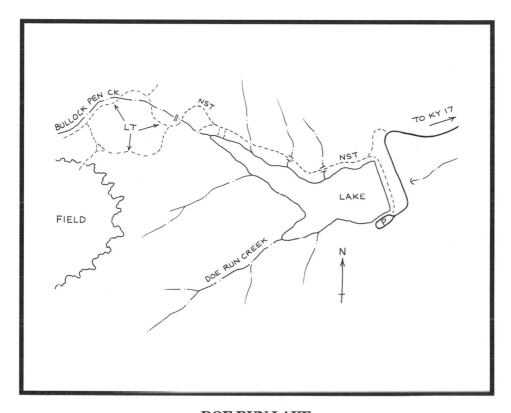

DOE RUN LAKE

37 BIG BONE LICK STATE PARK

Lakeside Loop
  Distance: 1.5 miles
  Terrain: hilly
  Walking time: 1 hour

Back-Country Loop
  Distance: 2.8 miles
  Terrain: hilly
  Walking Time: 2 hours

Famous for its sulfur springs and Pleistocene fossil excavations, **Big Bone Lick State Park** covers 500 acres of forested hill-country in northern Kentucky. A museum and diorama walk depict the natural history of the preserve and two hiking trails lead through a rich deciduous woodland that surrounds the Park's 7.5 acre lake. Big Bone Lick's 62-site campground is open the the public throughout the year.

Directions: From I-71, west of I-75, take Exit 72 and drive north on KY14. Proceed 2.3 miles and turn right on U.S. 42/127. Drive 3 miles and turn left on KY 338; the Park will be 2.9 miles ahead, on your left.

From I-75, take Exit 175 at Richwood and head west on KY 338 to the Park; the entrance will be 2.9 miles beyond the intersection with U.S. 42/127.

Routes: Access to the hiking trails at Big Bone Lick State Park is via the "nature trail parking lot" east of the entrance road (see map). While the hiking trails are currently un-named, we have designated two loops: the **Lakeside Loop (LSL)** and the **Back-Country Loop (BCL)**.

The **Lakeside Loop** exits the parking lot and climbs on to the dam via a long stairway. This 1.5 mile route then crosses the dam and begins an excursion around the Park's 7.5 acre lake. Stocked with bass, bluegill and catfish, the lake attracts fishermen throughout the year; birdwatchers will find great blue and green-backed herons along its shores and migrant waterfowl on its open waters during the spring and fall migrations. The dam itself offers a superb view of the surrounding hills and can be an excellent spot for hawk watching. White-tailed deer are often seen on the wooded meadow just east of the lake.

The **Back-Country Loop** also begins and ends at the "nature trail lot." Climb the stairway to the dam, cross the dam and continue straight ahead through the trail intersection, descending toward a stream channel. The 2.5 mile route turns southward, crosses a drainage and then begins a long, steady climb along the Park's eastern boundary. Nearing the ridgetop, the wide path turns westward and follows the edge of a cattle ranch, crossing the upper reaches of the Lake's feeder streams along the way. Hugging the Park boundary, the trail eventually turns back to the north and exits the forest near a water tower at the south end of the Campground (CG). Follow the east arm of the campground loop road and pick up the trail that descends toward the lake (see map), soon merging with the **Lakeside Loop (LSL)**. Hike northward along the west shore and descend the stairway to the parking lot.

A winter scene at Big Bone Lick

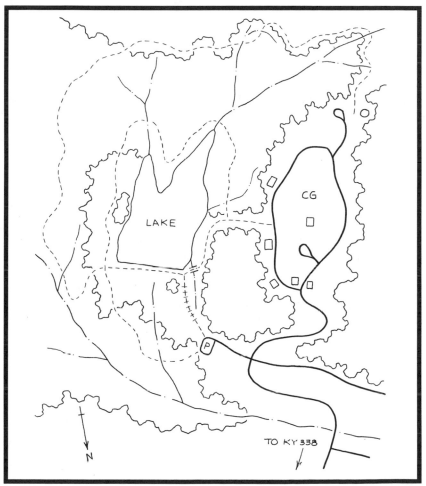

BIG BONE LICK STATE PARK

38 KINCAID LAKE STATE PARK

Combined Loop
  Distance: 2 miles
  Terrain: hilly
  Walking time: 1.5 hours

Nestled in the hills of northern Kentucky, **Kincaid Lake State Park** stretches along the south shore of a scenic, 183-acre oasis. The Lake itself attracts fishermen and boaters throughout the year and the Park's 84-site campground is open April through October. A 2.25 mile network of hiking trails provides access to a forested hillside south of the Recreation Area.

Directions: From I-75, take Exit 154, proceed eastward through Williamstown and pick up KY 22 east. Drive 15 miles and turn south on U.S. 27 to Falmouth. Turn left on KY 22 and then left on KY 159. The Park entrance will be 5 miles ahead, on your right. Proceed to the parking lot at the Recreation Center (R), which is south of the pool and west of the amphitheater (A).

Route: Follow the paved path that leaves the southwest corner of the lot and proceed to the hiking trail network via a trail that angles to the southeast, passing a shelter building (S). At the next intersection, turn left, hiking toward the campgrounds. Take the second trail on your right, gradually climbing above a stream and crossing numerous drainages along the way. Insects are abundant in this moist woodland and use of a repellent is strongly recommended; better yet, plan your visit during the fall or winter months.

Nearing the ridgetop the trail curves to the north and intersects a trail that leads to the maintenance area (see map). Continue straight ahead and you will soon reach a fork in the trail; either route descends toward the lake basin, rejoining near a marshy inlet. Cross the bridge and turn left at the trail intersection, returning to the recreation area via your original entry path (see map).

Approaching the ridgetop

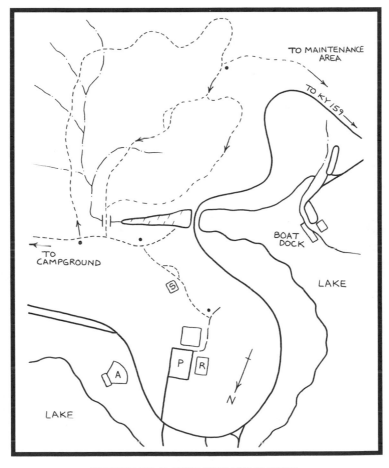

KINCAID LAKE STATE PARK

39 MULLINS WILDLIFE MANAGEMENT AREA

Jeep Trail
   Distance: 2.5 miles roundtrip
   Terrain: rolling; few hills
   Walking time: 1.5-2.0 hours

Mullins Wildlife Management Area, southwest of Walton, is devoid of spectacular scenery. There are no magnificent vistas, no rock-walled gorges, no natural arches and no breath-taking waterfalls. However, like many of the Wildlife Management Areas, this 266-acre preserve offers something that the State Parks and National Recreation Areas cannot often provide: solitude. With the exception of hunting season, Mullin's jeep trail and earthen paths are generally free of human visitors. Home to deer, raccoons, skunks, opossums, hawks and a variety of songbirds, this patchwork of fields and woodlands offers a peaceful escape for the naturalist during any season of the year.

Directions: From I-75, take Exit 171 and head east into Walton, Kentucky. Turn south on U.S. 25 and drive 2.7 miles; turn right (west) at the Wildlife Management Area sign and proceed 1.6 miles, crossing over I-75 along the way. Turn left on Courtney Road; the parking lot will be .2 mile, on your left.

Route: From the parking lot, hike southward on a jeep trail that leads across an open field (see map). Just over 1/4 mile from the lot, the trail angles to the right and begins a gradual descent to a stream crossing, passing beneath powerlines along the way.

   The path enters a parcel of deciduous forest, fords two branches of the creek and than ascends toward the southwest. After winding through an open woodland the trail skirts the edge of a large field and then angles sharply to the right (see map), re-entering the forest. Descending back to the primary stream, the path crosses a tributary and follows the main creek to a roadway at the edge of the Wildlife Area. Return to your car via the same route, completing a 2.5 mile roundtrip hike.

Mid summer at the Mullins Wildlife Area

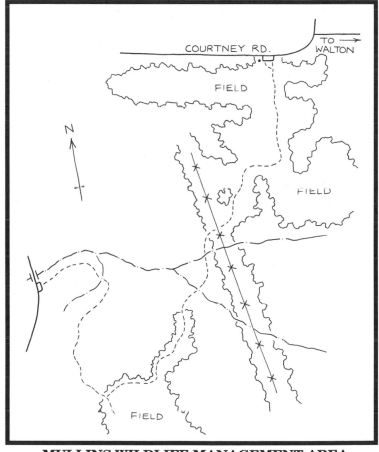

MULLINS WILDLIFE MANAGEMENT AREA

40 QUIET TRAILS STATE NATURE PRESERVE

Combined Loop Hike
  Distance: 2 miles
  Terrain: rolling; few hills
  Walking time: 1.5 hours

Whitetail Rest Trail
  Distance: 1.2 miles roundtrip
  Terrain: rolling
  Walking time: 1 hour

True to its name, **Quiet Trails State Nature Preserve** offers a peaceful retreat, far from large cities and interstate highways. Stretching above the west bank of the Licking River, this refuge, once an active farm, now greets the visitor with a mix of cedar groves, rolling meadows and second-third growth forest. A network of wide paths lead through these varied habitats and down to the Licking's floodplain.

Directions: From Cynthiana, head north on U.S. 27. Drive 10 miles and turn right (east) on KY 1284. Proceed 2.7 miles to an intersection at the Sunrise General Store; cross straight through the intersection, heading north on Pughs Ferry Road. Bear left at the Moore's Mill Road junction (.6 miles beyond the General Store intersection) and continue another 1.2 miles on Pughs Ferry Road to the Nature Preserve lot, on your right.

Routes: Combined Loop Hike (2 miles). From the lot, hike eastward on the **Center Trail (CNT)** which follows the treeline at the north edge of a large meadow (see map). Bypass cutoffs to the meadow, remaining on the wide, **Center Trail** which passes two old farm ponds and soon intersects the **Cedar Trail (CDT)** and **Sassafras Trail (SFT)**. Bear left on the latter which makes a broad curve to the north, entering the forest and crossing several streambeds along the way.

Return to the **Center Trail**, turn left and hike a short distance to the Preserve's old barn (B). Beyond this rustic structure, the **Center Trail** descends to a picnic shelter (S) near the west bank of the Licking River.

For your return route, pick up the **Deep Hollow Trail (DHT)** which cuts away from the **Center Trail** and climbs along a forest stream, exiting the woods at the south edge of the central meadow (see map).

Whitetail Rest Trail (WTR). This trail, 1.2 miles roundtrip, is a series of three loops. Hiking northward from the parking lot, follow the trail loops counterclockwise as each is encountered (see map). The first two loops wind along the edge of small meadows on either side of an old barn (B) while the terminal loop is entirely within the forest. The trail is named for whitetail deer, the common eastern species, which rest in the forest by day and emerge to browse on the meadows as dusk envelopes the refuge.

*An old barn
at Quiet Trails*

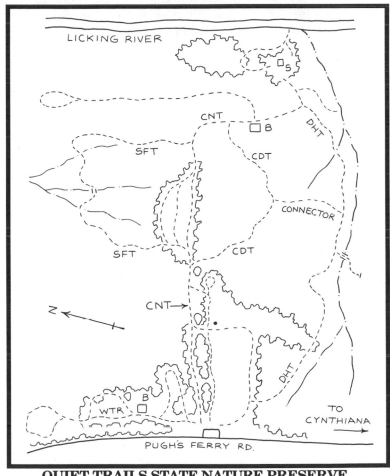

QUIET TRAILS STATE NATURE PRESERVE

127

41 JOHN A. KLEBER WILDLIFE MANAGEMENT AREA

Elm Fork Trail
  Distance: 6 miles roundtrip
  Terrain: rolling
  Walking time: 4 hours

Oakland Branch to Elm Fork
  Distance: 3 miles roundtrip
  Terrain: rolling
  Walking time: 2 hours

Mt. Vernon Ridge Trail
  Distance: 3.4 miles roundtrip
  Terrain: rolling
  Walking time: 2.5 hours

The **John A. Kleber Wildlife Management Area**, a mosaic of forest and meadow, stretches along the Cedar Creek Valley, 14 miles northwest of Georgetown, Kentucky. This "U-shaped" preserve covers 2228 acres in Owen and Franklin Counties and is accessed by three jeep roads. Hikers can stroll atop the backbone of Mt. Vernon Ridge or meander along the channel of Elm Fork and naturalists will find a superb variety of flora and fauna at this secluded refuge.

Directions: From Georgetown, head west on U.S. 460. Drive 1 mile beyond the city limits and turn right (north) on KY 227. Proceed 8 miles and turn left (west) on KY 368. Oakland Branch Road will be 5 miles ahead and Hall Branch Road is another .2 mile. The Wildlife Area Headquarters (HQ) is 2 miles northeast of the Halls Branch junction, on KY 368 (see map).

Routes: Elm Fork Trail (our terminology). This 3 mile jeep road (6 miles roundtrip) leaves the north side of KY 368, just southeast of the Headquarters Area (see map). Crossing open meadows and parcels of forest, this graveled path undulates above the north bank of Elm Fork, ending at the town of Harmony. Birding can be excellent along this trail and children will enjoy scouting the puddles and sidestreams for the numerous frogs, toads and salamanders that inhabit the refuge. Return to your car via the same route.

Oakland Branch Trail (our terminology). This 1.5 mile route (3 miles roundtrip) cuts north from Oakland Branch Road, less than 1/4 mile east of KY 368 (see map). Following the crest of a low ridge, this old jeep road snakes through open woodlands and ends on the south bank of Elm Fork; if the water level is low enough to allow safe crossing, hikers can ford the creek and pick up the **Elm Fork Trail** on the north bank. The return route to Oakland Branch Road is via the same jeep path.

128

*Gravel roads
provide access to
the Wildlife Area*

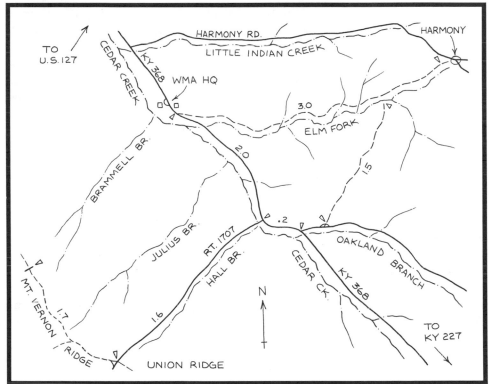

JOHN A. KLEBER WILDLIFE MANAGEMENT AREA

Mt. Vernon Ridge Trail (our terminology). This jeep road angles north-westward from Halls Branch Road (Rt. 1707), 1.6 miles west of KY 368 (see map). The trail follows the crest of the ridge and yields broad views across the Cedar Creek Valley. Private property is encountered after hiking 1.7 miles; return to your car from this point, completing a roundtrip excursion of 3.4 miles.

42 BLUE LICKS BATTLEFIELD STATE PARK

Combined Loop Hike
Distance: 1.5 miles
Terrain: hilly
Walking time: 1 hour

Blue Licks Battlefield State Park, 26 miles southwest of Maysville, Kentucky, is a site of historic and prehistoric significance. Before the first human Americans set foot in Kentucky, mastadons, bison and other Pleistocene mammals were attracted to the natural "salt licks" that characterize this portion of the Licking River Valley. Many centuries later, during the 1800s, these same mineral springs became a human gathering place, offering a cool summer retreat and "curative waters."

However, the Valley is most famous for the Battle of Blue Licks, the last battle of the Revolutionary War to be fought in Kentucky. On August 19, 1782, a regiment of the Kentucky militia were soundly routed by British and Indian forces, led by Captain William Caldwell. Daniel Boone, a Lieutenant Colonel, and his son, Israel, fought for the Kentucky militia; Israel was killed in the battle.

Directions: From I-75 at Lexington, take Exit 113 and head northeast on U.S. 68. The Park will be 40 miles ahead. Park in the lot just north of the gift shop (GS).

Route: Hiking at the State Park is limited to a 1.5 mile loop that begins and ends at the gift shop (GS) parking lot (see map). Hike southward on the **Buffalo Trace Trail (BT)** which leads through the Park's Nature Preserve; a side trail leads out to a small meadow which harbors Short's goldenrod. This endangered plant, endemic to the area, is found only within a 2 mile radius of the Park.

Turn right along the main Park road and then left on the campground (CG) entrance road. Pick up the trail that leads westward from the check-in area, descending toward the Licking River. The path curves north along the River's east bank, crossing several side streams, and then turns eastward for a gradual ascent to a picnic area; be sure to bear left at a fork in the trail (see map). Beyond the shelter (S), a final short stairway leads back to the gift shop lot.

130

Human plans must often yield to nature's handiwork

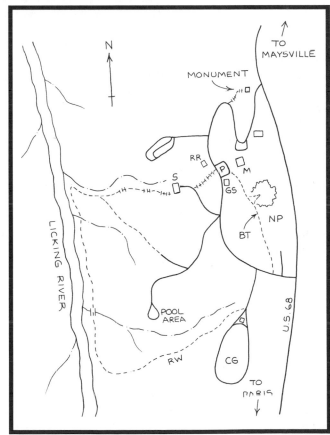

BLUE LICKS BATTLEFIELD STATE PARK

43 CARTER CAVES STATE RESORT PARK

Red Trail Loop
  Distance: 3.25 miles
  Terrain: hilly
  Walking time: 2 hours

Blue-Red Loop
  Distance: 1.5 miles
  Terrain: hilly
  Walking time: 1 hour

Natural Bridge Trail
  Distance: .5 mile
  Terrain: hilly
  Walking time: .5 hour

Cascade Nature Trail
  Distance: .8 mile
  Terrain: hilly
  Walking time: .75 hour

Simon Kenton Trail (to Shangra La Arch)
  Distance: 1 mile roundtrip
  Terrain: hilly
  Walking time: .75 hour

Harboring over 200 caves, Carter County has long been a mecca for spelunkers and other students of nature. Twenty of these caverns are protected withing the boundaries of **Carter Caves State Resort Park**, established in 1946.

The Park offers three cave tours, including a 1.25 hour excursion through Cascade Cave, the County's largest, which features a 30-foot underground waterfall. While these tours attract most of the visitors, the Park also offers over 6 miles of hiking trails which lead past a spectacular collection of rock bluffs, recessed caves and natural bridges.

Directions: From I-64, take Exit #161. Cross to the north side of the highway and proceed east on U.S. 60 for a short distance. Turn north on Ky 182 and you will soon descend into the Tygart Creek valley; the Park entrance will be on your left, just after crossing the Creek (approximately 3 miles north of U.S. 60).

Routes: Red Trail Loop (RT). This 3.4 mile loop is the longest trail in the Park and is easily accessed from a number of parking areas; we suggest that you leave your car at the **Welcome Center (WC)** lot . Cross the road and ascend a short stairway just north of **Saltpetre Cave (SC)**. Turn left (south) on the **Red Trail**, soon climbing atop the rock bluffs and winding to the southeast. Just east of the cabin area, the trail descends past **Fern Bridge (FB)**, a fine recessed cave in the sandstone that caps the Park's central plateau.

Nearing Tygart Creek, the **Red Trail** curves to the northwest, crosses several drainages and eventually leads above the north shore of **Smokey Valley Lake**. Bypass cutoffs to the **Blue Trail (BT)**, pass behind the Park Lodge (L) and descend to **Smokey Bridge (SB)**, the largest natural bridge in Kentucky. From this spectacular landform, the **Red Trail** leads northward

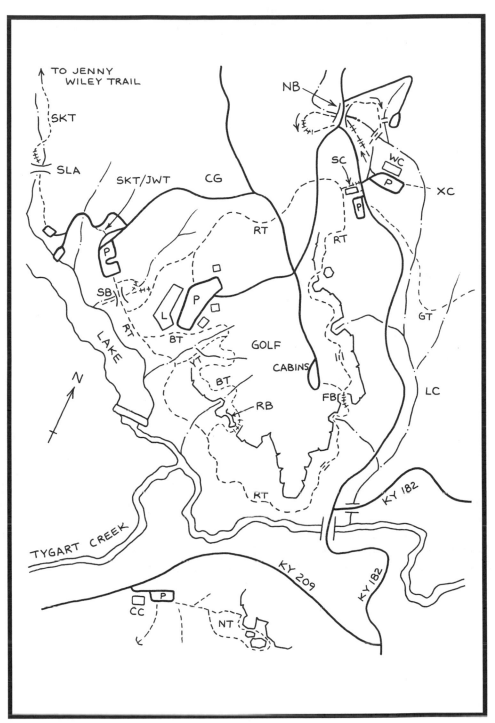

CARTER CAVES STATE RESORT PARK

above a sidestream, climbing toward the Park's Campground (CG). This section of the trail is open to horsemen and can be nearly impassable after periods of wet weather.

After crossing two roadways, the **Red Trail** leads back to the **Saltpetre Cave (SC)**; turn left, descend the stairway and cross to the **Welcome Center** lot.

Blue-Red Loop. This combined route yields a hike of 1.5 miles. Pick up the **Blue Trail (BT)** near the south edge of the Lodge (L) parking lot and hike eastward, passing a pool. Turning southward, the trail winds atop the edge of the central plateau, crossing several drainages and skirting the Park's golf course. Bypass the **Yellow Trail (YT)** and follow the **Blue Trail** to **Raven Bridge (RB)**, which has eroded from the sandstone bluffs. Descend through the rock wall and hike down to the **Red Trail (RT)**; turn right for a short walk back to the Lodge area.

Natural Bridge Trail. This .5 mile, figure-8 route begins and ends at the **Welcome Center (WC)**. Descend a paved driveway (just west of the Center building) and angle onto a trail that hugs the valley wall and soon passes under the **Carter Caves Natural Bridge (NB)**. This impessive span, 180 feet wide, is the only natural bridge in Kentucky which supports a paved roadway.

After passing through this natural tunnel the path curves southward and eastward, climbing to the road. Cross the bridge, turn right and descend back to the stream, completing the double-loop route.

Cascade Nature Trail (NT). This .8 mile loop begins and ends at the **Cascade Cave (CC)** parking lot on the south side of Ky 209, .7 mile west of Ky 182 (see map). Hike eastward from the lot, bypassing side trails and soon reaching a scenic box canyon, bordered by sandstone cliffs and recessed caves. After winding past (and through) these rock formations, the trail curves back to the west, descends through the forest and completes its loop.

Simon Kenton Trail (SKT). This 9 mile trail begins at the parking lot just north of the **Smokey Bridge (SB)** and ends at the **Jenny Wiley Trail**, a 163 mile path that stretches from the Ohio River to Jenny Wiley State Resort Park (see Chapter II and Hiking Area 56). Day hikers can use this trail to reach the **Shangra La Arch (SLA)**, a roundtrip distance of 1 mile.

The trailhead for the **Simon Kenton Trail** (and for access to the **Jenny Wiley Trail**) is just north of the parking lot (see map). The path soon intersects a park road; turn left and hike along the roadway, bearing right as you near **Smokey Valley Lake**. The trail exits a small lot and leads to the northwest, climbing along a side stream to the natural arch. Return to the parking area via the same route.

Approaching the Natural Bridge

Inside, looking Out

Michael Tygart Loop
  Distance: 7 miles
  Terrain: hilly
  Walking time: 4.5 hours

Fern Valley Interpretive Trail
  Distance: 1.1 mile
  Terrain: rolling
  Walking time: .75 hour

Greenbo Lake, created by damming three tributaries of the Little Sandy River, is the centerpiece of a beautiful **State Resort Park** in northeastern Kentucky. Characterized by 3330 acres of forested hills and valleys, the Park offers over 9 miles of hiking trails.

White-tailed deer are abundant here, often foraging along the roadways, and historic structures compliment the natural scenery of this wooded retreat. Of particular interest is the old **Buffalo Furnace (F)**, which operated from 1851 to 1875 and supplied iron for the Union Army during the Civil War.

Directions: From I-64, take Exit 172 and head north on Ky 1. Drive almost 15 miles and turn left (west) on Ky 1711; the Park will be 2 miles ahead.

From U.S. 23, northwest of Ashland, turn south on Ky 1 and drive 7.7 miles to Ky 1711; turn right on Ky 1711 and proceed 2 miles to the Park.

Routes: Michael Tygart Loop. The **Michael Tygart Trail (MTT)** is a 24 mile back-country trail that begins at the **Greenbo Lake State Resort Park** Lodge (L) and heads west to intersect the **Jenny Wiley Trail**, a 163 mile path that stretches from the Ohio River, at South Portsmouth, to Jenny Wiley State Restort Park, near Prestonsburg, Kentucky. A section of the **Michael Tygart Trail** within the Park can be combined with the **Michael Tygart Loop Trail (TLT)** to yield a day hike of 7 miles.

Park at the Boat Dock and hike eastward on the gravel road that parallels the lakeshore; pick up the **Tygart Loop Trail** at the end of this lane and enter the forest, soon curving northward to negotiate a drainage. Climbing above Greenbo Lake, the trail continues eastward and then descends along the Pruitt Fork inlet. Watch for wood ducks in this area.

Curving westward, the **Tygart Loop Trail** begins a long, gradual ascent through the Pruitt Fork Valley. Deer are often spotted in the clearings and both ruffed grouse and pileated woodpeckers are common in this secluded forest. Abandoned, 19th Century homesteads will also be encountered along the trail. Turn left on Raccoon Ridge Road, proceed to the second lane on your left and hike eastward on the **Michael Tygart Trail (MTT)**. This section of the trail runs atop a ridge that divides the Claylick and Buffalo Valleys, gradually descending toward the central Park road. Emerging near a cemetery (C), turn left and return to the Boat Dock lot (see map).

Fern Valley Interpretive Trail (FVT). Those desiring a shorter hike should consider this 1.1 mile, self-guided nature trail. The loop is accessed

An abandoned homestead along the Tygart Loop Trail

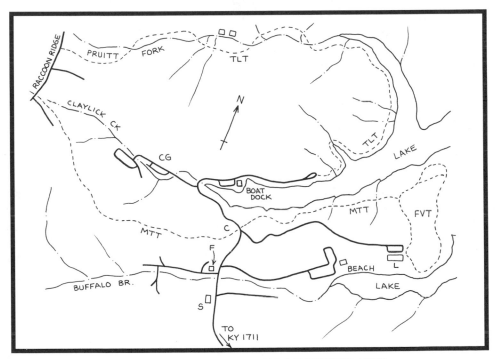

GREENBO LAKE STATE RESORT PARK

at the east end of the Lodge (L) parking lot. Sixteen points of interest are spaced along the trail and guidebooks are available at the front desk in the Lodge. The trail is designed to introduce visitors to the flora and fauna of northeastern Kentucky.

45 JESSE STUART STATE NATURE PRESERVE

Combined Loop Hike
 Distance: 2 miles
 Terrain: hilly
 Walking time: 1.5 hours

Jesse Stuart, 1906-1984, Kentucky's Poet Laureate and a nominee for the Pulitzer Prize in Poetry in 1977, lived much of his life in "W Hollow," a short distance south of the Ohio River. Born in this secluded valley, Stuart incorporated its rich natural heritage into most of his writings. It is thus fitting that Kentucky has honored his life's work by setting aside 703 acres of W Hollow as the **Jesse Stuart State Nature Preserve**, protecting the valley's native flora and fauna.

A network of hiking trails provides access to the Preserve's western section, running along forest streams and atop Seaton Ridge. Sunny meadows are spaced along the route and the remnants of an old homestead compliment the natural scenery.

Directions: From I-64, just north of Grayson, take Exit 172 and head north on KY 1. Drive 20.4 miles and turn left on W Hollow Road; an historic marker honoring Jesse Stuart is at this intersection. Proceed 1.6 miles to the refuge lot, on your right.

Route: A 2 mile loop hike can be achieved by combining sections of several trails. From the parking lot, hike northwestward on a wide path that crosses a meadow and then climbs onto the ridge via a broad switchback. Atop the ridge you will intersect an old jeep road (and gas pipeline swath); turn left and walk northward to a clearing where a cabin (C) and barn (B) mark the site of an old homestead.

Continue past these structures and then bear right at the private property entrance, staying atop the ridge. At the next intersection, bear left, cross through a meadow and follow the **Seaton Ridge Trail (SRT)** to an overlook (V) of the Ohio River Valley.

Backtrack to the old homestead and turn left (east) on the **Coon Den Hollow Trail (CDH)**, which enters the forest just south of the barn (B) and makes a gradual descent to a stream crossing. Bypass the **Shingle Mill Hollow Trail (SMH)**, cross the creek and follow the trail as it snakes southward and then westward, climbing back to the jeep road. Cross this broad path, descend to another stream bed and then hike up to the parking lot.

*An old homestead
sits atop the ridge*

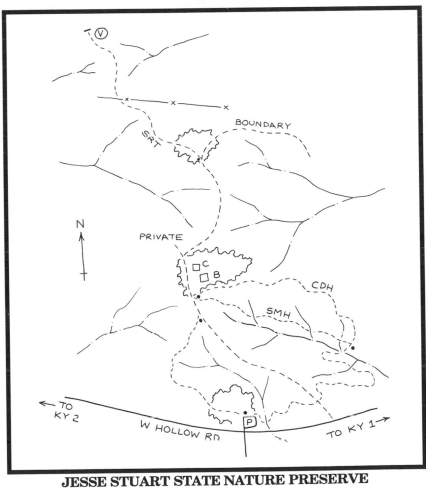

JESSE STUART STATE NATURE PRESERVE

VIII. HIKING AREAS OF EASTERN KENTUCKY

46. Grayson Lake
47. Cave Run Lake-Pioneer Weapons Area and Vicinity
48. Spencer-Morton Preserve
49. Red River Gorge Nat. Recreation Area
50. Natural Bridge State Resort Park
51. Central Kentucky Wildlife Mgmt. Area
52. Berea College Forest
53. Turkey Foot Recreation Area
54. Buckhorn Lake State Resort Park
55. Paintsville Lake
56. Jenny Wiley State Resort Park
57. Levi Jackson Wilderness Road State Park
58. Redbird Crest Trail
59. Bad Branch State Nature Preserve
60. Kingdom Come State Park
61. Pine Mountain State Resort Park
62. Cumberland Gap Nat. Historic Park

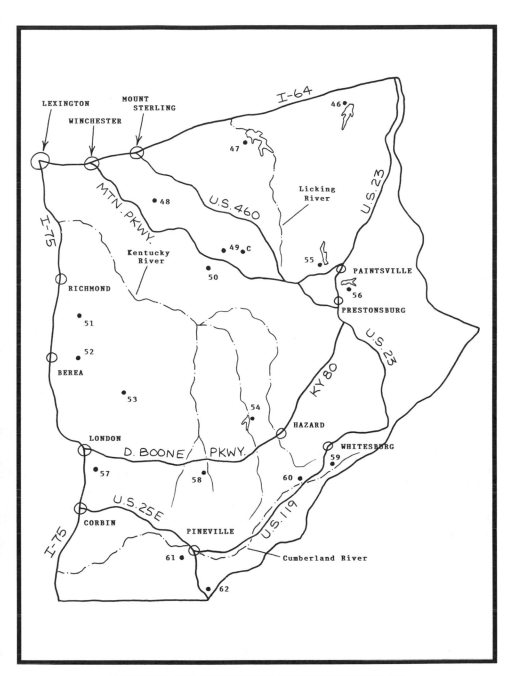

HIKING AREAS OF EASTERN KENTUCKY

Grayson Lake Nature Trail
  Distance: 1.75 miles
  Terrain: hilly
  Walking time: 1.5 hours

Deer Creek Trail
  Distance: 4 miles roundtrip
  Terrain: rolling; one steep hill
  Walking time: 2.5 hours

Grayson Lake, a flood-control reservoir on the Little Sandy River, was a project of the U.S. Army Corps of Engineers, completed in April of 1969. A State Park campground (CG) is located off KY 7, west of the Lake, and a 14,763 acre Wildlife Management Area (WMA) stretches along the eastern shore.

The **Grayson Lake Nature Trail (NT)** offers a scenic, 1.75 mile hike below the Dam and adventurous trekkers may want to explore the Wildlife Management Area via a network of old boy scout trails.

Directions: From I-64, take Exit 172 and head south on KY 7. Drive 6.5 miles to KY 1496, which angles to the southeast (see map). Those heading to the Wildlife Management Area should turn left on KY 1496 and proceed 2 miles to the Camp Webb (CW) entry road; park in the lot on the east bank of Deer Creek.

To reach the Grayson Lake Nature Trail, stay on KY 7, cross the Dam and then turn right, descending to parking lots along the River (see map).

Routes: Grayson Lake Nature Trail (NT). This well-engineered, 1.75 mile loop trail is accessed from several lots below the Grayson Lake Dam (see map). Hike it counterclockwise, climbing onto a wooded ridge via several switchbacks. Leveling off atop the ridge, the trail soon reaches a picnic shelter and then angles to the left, descending toward the Little Sandy River. After squeezing through a rock formation, the trail turns upstream, undulating above the east bank and fording several small creeks.

The trail curves westward and then southward, dropping to the join a wide path that parallels the River and leads back to picnic areas below the Dam. This section of the trail, passing rock cliffs that tower above the stream, is especially scenic.

Deer Creek Trail (DCT). As discussed above, the Grayson Lake Wildlife Management Area, east of the Lake, is accessed by a network of old scout trails. At the time of our visit, these trails and their intersections were not well marked and we thus recommend this area for experienced hikers only.

The **Deer Creek Trail** heads upstream through a broad valley, crossing streamside meadows and open woodlands. Bear left (straight) at the first trail intersection and continue upstream for another mile, eventually leaving the creek and climbing onto a ridge. Turn left at the top of the ridge, bypass the first cutoff on your right and proceed to overlooks above a

*The Grayson Lake
Nature Trail*

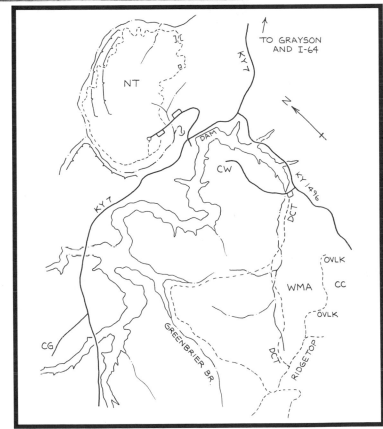

**GRAYSON
LAKE**

large clearcut area (CC). While this trail originally continued northward to intersect KY 1496, it is now overgrown and we recommend that you backtrack to your car via the **Deer Creek Trail**. Your roundtrip hike will total 4 miles.

47 CAVE RUN LAKE - PIONEER WEAPONS AREA AND VICINITY

Distance: Dayhikes of 2.5 to 11.7 miles
Terrain: mostly hilly; some rolling terrain atop ridges and in valleys
Walking time: Dayhikes of 2 to 8 hours

Flanked by Recreation Areas and surrounded by forested hills of the Appalachian Plateau, **Cave Run Lake** is the jewel of northeastern Kentucky. This scenic, 8270 acre reservoir was created by damming the Licking River, a U.S. Army Corps of Engineers project, completed in 1974.

Hiking trails are plentiful throughout the region, including a 60-mile segment of the **Sheltowee Trace Trail (STT)**, which passes north and west of the Lake. We have grouped the dayhikes of the Cave Run Lake region into three areas: Trails North of Cave Run Lake, the Pioneer Weapons Area and Trails from Clear Creek Lake.

Directions: From I-64, take Exit 123 and head east on U.S. 60. Drive 6.5 miles to the town of Salt Lick (see overview map).

Hikes originating at **Clear Creek Lake (CCL)** are accessed from a lot at the east end of the lake, off Forest Road 129, 2 miles east of KY 211.

Dayhikes in the **Pioneer Weapons Area** are accessed from Forest Roads 918 and 918A, north of Forest Road 129 and west of Cave Run Lake.

The **Caney Loop Trail** originates at the Stoney Cove Picnic Area (SC), off KY 826, just south of the Cave Run Lake Dam.

To reach the **Big Limestone Trail (BLT)**, proceed east on U.S. 60 to the west edge of Morehead, Kentucky. Turn south on KY 519, drive 3.7 miles and turn right on KY 1274. Proceed 1.1 mile and turn right on Forest Road 16. Another .7 mile brings you to Forest Road 964; turn right, winding upward and northwestward for 1.6 miles to the access lot.

144

Looking northeast from the Tater Knob fire tower

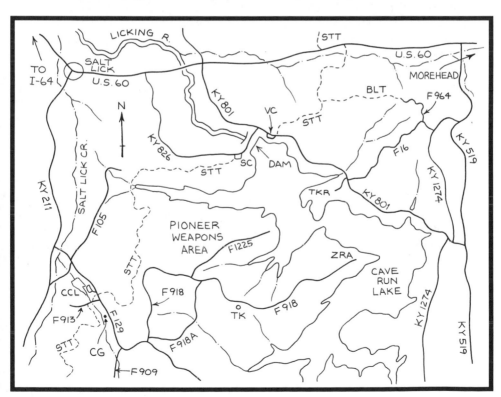

**CAVE RUN LAKE/PIONEER WEAPONS AREA & VICINITY
(OVERVIEW MAP)**

Routes: There are a tremendous number of potential dayhikes in the vicinity of Cave Run Lake. As discussed above, we have grouped our recommendations within three areas: Trails North of Cave Run Lake, the Pioneer Weapons Area and Trails from Clear Creek Lake. Trails within the Zilpo (ZRA) and Twin Knob (TKR) Recreation Areas, both of which charge entry fees, have not been included.

TRAILS NORTH OF CAVE RUN LAKE

Big Limestone Trail (BLT). This scenic trail is a westward extension of Forest Road 964, running atop the ridge that divides the Triplett Creek and Scott Creek watersheds, north of Cave Run Lake. From the access lot at the gated, west end of Road 964, the **Big Limestone Trail** (designated Forest Trail 109) winds westward for 2.5 miles to joint the **Sheltowee Trace Trail (STT)**. Broad views to the north and south are spaced along the route and dayhikers may want to plan a roundtrip excursion to Limestone Knob (LK, elevation 1435 feet), which is 1.75 miles from the F.R. 964 trailhead (a roundtrip hike of 3.5 miles). Plan for 2.5 hours of walking time on this dayhike.

Caney Loop Trail (CLT). This 11.7 mile hike begins and ends at the Stoney Cove Picnic Area (SC) just south of the Cave Run Lake Dam. From the large parking lot, hike southward on Forest Road 1062, climbing to the forest edge. Turn left on a trail that winds above the Caney Creek inlet of Cave Run Lake, crossing numerous drainages along the way. This trail eventually turns northward and intersects the **Sheltowee Trace Trail (STT)**. Turn right and follow this renowned path back to Stoney Cove. Be advised that this strenuous dayhike crosses hilly terrain and takes at least 7-8 hours to complete; we recommend it for fit and experienced hikers only.

PIONEER WEAPONS AREA

This 7480 acre Wildlife Management Area, just west of Cave Run Lake, was set aside as a hunting grounds where 18th Century weapons (bow and arrow, black-powder firearms, etc.) must be used. During the rest of the year, this preserve offers an excellent network of hiking trails. We suggest the following dayhikes:

Forest Road 918 to Tater Knob Tower. This 5.5 mile (roundtrip) hike begins at a gravelled pulloff on Forest Road 918, .8 mile north of Forest Road 129. Hike eastward on the **Buck Creek Trail (118)**, descending along the stream. Cross Road 918A and continue another mile to the **Tater Knob Trail (104)** junction; a relatively short but steep climb via **104** takes you up to the Tater Knob (TK) lot where a lung-busting stairway ascends to the fire tower. From its lookout platform, visitors are treated to a panoramic view of the Cave Run region. Return to Forest Road 918 via the same route. Hikers should plan at least 4 hours for this strenuous dayhike.

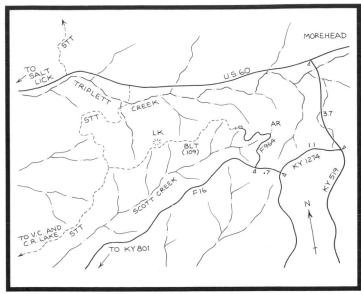

BIG LIMESTONE TRAIL

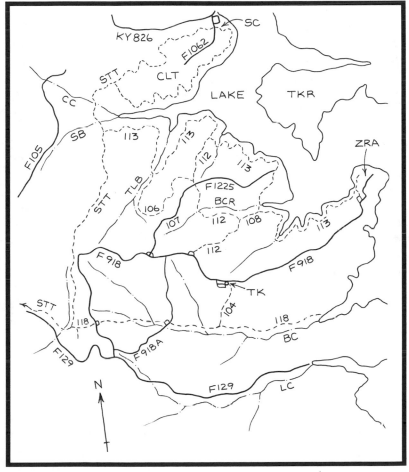

CANEY LOOP TRAIL

PIONEER WEAPONS AREA

Combined Loop Hike (112-108-113-112). This 7.5 mile route, covering hilly terrain, will take almost 5 hours hike. The loop begins along Forest Road 918, a short distance east of the 918A junction, where the **Cave Run Trail (112)** heads northeast, beginning a long descent to Big Cave Run Creek (BCR). Nearing the creek, turn right on **Trail 108** which soon intersects the **Buckskin Trail (113)**. Turn left and follow this trail as it winds along and above the west shore of Cave Run Lake. Bypass the junction with the **Cross Over Trail (107; old Forest Road 1225)** and continue northwestward to the northern terminus of the **Cave Run Trail (112)**. Turn left and follow this trail back to Road 918 (see map, page 147).

Cross Over Trail (107; old Forest Road 1225). Since it follows the crest of a ridge, this trail, which begins on Forest Road 918 (see map, page 147) is a pleasant route for dayhikers. The entire roundtrip distance to the **Buckskin Trail (113)** junction is 3.5 miles; plan 2-2.5 hours for this dayhike.

TRAILS FROM CLEAR CREEK LAKE

A large parking lot at the east end of Clear Creek Lake, off Forest Road 129, serves as a trailhead for several dayhikes:

Clear Creek Trail (103). From the trailhead lot, hike southward on the **Sheltowee Trace Trail (STT)** to Forest Road 913. Turn right and follow this gravel road toward the southwest. Just past the second stream crossing, turn right on the **Clear Creek Trail** which parallels the south shore of the lake to the Dam. Return via the same route, completing a roundtrip hike of 2.5 miles; plan 2 hours for this hike.

Sheltowee Trace Trail (STT) to Stoney Cove (SC). By using two cars, or by arranging transportation, one can plan a 9.6 mile dayhike (one-way) from the Clear Creek Lake trailhead to the Stoney Cove Picnic Area at the south end of the Cave Run Lake Dam (see maps, pages 145 & 147). This route ascends along the Buck Branch of Clear Creek, levels out atop a ridge and then descends to cross Caney Creek before winding northeastward to Stoney Cove. Hikers should plan at least 6 hours for this strenuous excursion.

Sheltowee Trace Trail (STT) to Carrington Rocks (CR). A two mile section of the **Sheltowee Trace Trail** (formerly known as the Carrington Rock Trail) leads southward from the Clear Creek Lake Area to Forest Road 908 (see map). The trail first leads eastward along Clear Creek (jogging to the south as it crosses Forest Road 913); nearing the Campground (CG), the **Sheltowee Trace Trail** curves back to the west and climbs onto a ridge. For the next 1.4 miles, the trail stays near the crest of the ridge, heading SSW. The route passes a natural arch (NA), crosses Road 906 and soon intersects Forest Road 908. Turn right (west) on this road which snakes westward to Carrington Rock. Most of this famous overlook is privately owned but adventurous hikers can ascend its eastern edge for a magnificent view of the Cave Run region. Return via the same route for a total hike of 5.5 miles.

148

Clear Creek Lake

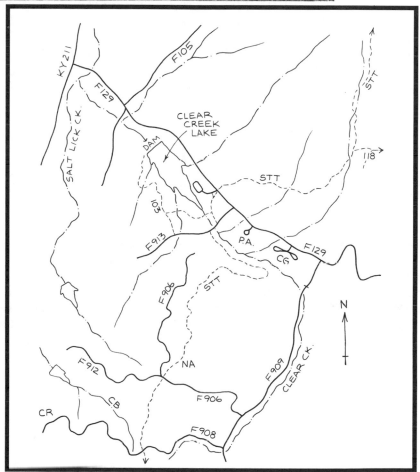

TRAILS FROM CLEAR CREEK LAKE

48 SPENCER-MORTON PRESERVE

Pilot Knob Trail
  Distance: 1.5 miles roundtrip
  Terrain: hilly; steep areas
  Walking time: 2 hours

Rising to 1400 feet, **Pilot Knob** stands almost 730 feet above the surrounding landscape of Powell County, yielding broad views to the south and west. Indeed, it is reported that Daniel Boone first surveyed the "flat lands" of the Kentucky bluegrass region from this lofty perch on June 7, 1769.

Capped by Pennsylvanian sandstone, Pilot Knob is an "outlier" of the Appalachian Plateau, dissected from its western edge by the forces of erosion. The Knob is now protected within the 308 acre **Spencer-Morton Preserve**, purchased with the assistance of the Kentucky Chapter of the Nature Conservancy, in 1976, and managed by the Division of Natural Areas of Eastern Kentucky University.

The climb to the summit of Pilot Knob is steep and strenuous; we recommend the trail for fit and experienced hikers and, due to the rugged terrain and unguarded cliffs, the route is not recommended for families with young children.

Directions: From the Mountain Parkway, east of Winchester, take Exit 16, proceed to the south side of the highway and head west on KY 15. Drive 3 miles and turn right (north) on a road that crosses over the Parkway and leads toward Pilot Knob. The parking lot for the Spencer-Morton Preserve will be at the end of this road (1.4 miles north of KY 15).

Route: From the graveled lot, a trail leads northeastward, passing a State Nature Preserve sign and crossing a stream. Bypass the cutoff on your left and enter the Preserve where a trailhead sign and brochure dispenser mark the boundary.

The **Pilot Knob Trail (PKT)** continues northeastward while the **Millstone Quarry Trail (MQT)** branches to the east. Stay on the **Pilot Knob Trail** and begin a steady, .75 mile climb to the summit. The route is strenuous, with many steep areas and only modest use of switchbacks. An oak-hickory forest dominates the flanks of Pilot Knob, with groves of Virginia pine appearing in disturbed areas. Dogwoods, redbuds and tulip trees are also found throughout the woodland.

Nearing the summit, the trail winds past ledges of Pennsylvanian sandstone, an erosion-resistant rock that caps the Knob. Recessed caves, often the precursors of natural bridges and arches, will be noted in the sandstone wall. Atop the uppermost ledge is a forest of chestnut oak, blackjack oak, Virginia pine and mountain laurel; these trees and shrubs are tolerant of the thin, dry soil that covers the rocky summit.

Looking southwest from Pilot Knob

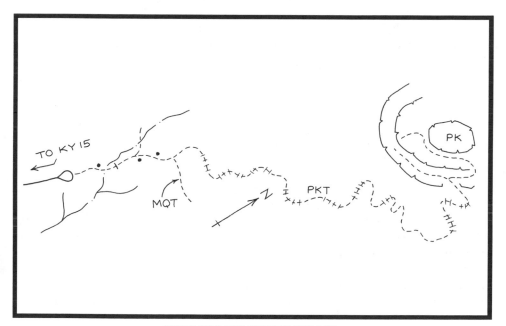

THE PILOT KNOB TRAIL

Walk out to an overlook at the southwestern edge of the Knob for a spectacular view of the Appalachian Plateau to the south and of the Outer Bluegrass Belt to the west. Other "knobs" can be seen along the boundary of these two geologic provinces.

Return to your car via the same route, completing a roundtrip hike of 1.5 miles.

49 RED RIVER GORGE
NATIONAL RECREATION AREA

Courthouse Rock via Trail 204
  Distance: 3 miles roundtrip
  Terrain: rolling
  Walking time: 2 hours

Gray's Arch via Trail 205
  Distance: 2.5 miles roundtrip
  Terrain: hilly
  Walking time: 1.75 hours

Loop Hike: 227-221-223
  Distance: 4 miles
  Terrain: hilly
  Walking time: 3 hours

Loop Hike: 220-221-223-226
  Distance: 6 miles
  Terrain: hilly
  Walking time: 4 hours

Rock Bridge Loop (207)
  Distance: 1.5 miles
  Terrain: hilly
  Walking time: 1 hour

Rough Trail (221)
  Distance: 8.4 miles (one way)
  Terrain: hilly
  Walking time: 6 hours

The **Red River**, a major tributary of the Kentucky River, rises in eastern Kentucky and flows westward across the Appalachian Plateau. In Wolfe, Menifee and Powell Counties, the River has carved a spectacular gorge, slicing through the varied rock strata of the Plateau and creating a scenic landscape of natural bridges, waterfalls, rock towers and steep, rugged cliffs. Shaded, moist ravines are adorned with groves of eastern hemlock and dense rhododendron thickets while a mixed forest of oak, hickory and pine cloaks the drier areas.

A **National Recreation Area** now encompasses the south wall of **Red River Gorge**, protecting its scenic wonders for future generations of hikers and naturalists. Accessed by a fine network of forest roads and hiking trails, the preserve is a mecca for back-country enthusiasts. The **Clifty Wilderness Area** stretches eastward from KY 715, extending protection to the upper gorge (see Chapter II).

Directions: From the Mountain Parkway, southeast of Winchester, take the Slade Exit (Exit 33). Cross to the north side of the Parkway and follow KY 15 to the trailhead areas, as illustrated on the map.

  Tunnel Ridge Road (TRR) provides access to many of the trailheads. This gravel road cuts north from KY 15, 3.2 miles east of the Slade Exit.

  The **Koomer Ridge Campground (KRCG)**, itself the starting point for several trails, is on the north side of KY 15, 4.9 miles east of the Exit 33.

  Rock Bridge Road (RBR), a 3 mile gravel road, cuts east from KY 715, .4 miles north of KY 15.

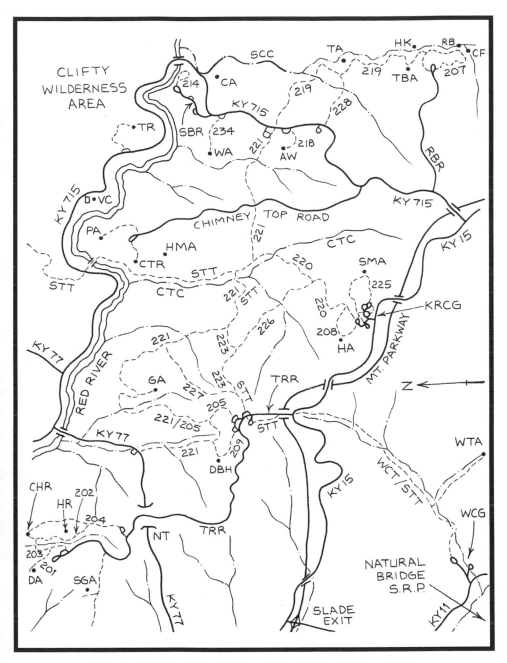

RED RIVER GORGE NAT. RECREATION AREA

Chimney Top Road, also a 3 mile gravel road, angles NNW from KY 715, 2.1 miles north of KY 15.

Numerous trailheads are spaced along **KY 715** and the **Rough Trail (221)** can also be accessed from **KY 77**, east of the Nada Tunnel (NT).

Routes: There are numerous potential dayhikes within Red River Gorge, including a portion of the **Sheltowee Trace Trail (STT)** which runs SSW to NNE through the Recreation Area (see map). Persons planning long dayhikes or backpacking trips in the Gorge should obtain 7.5 minute Quadrangle maps from the U.S. Geological Survey (available at most map stores and outdoor recreation shops); the Slade and Pomeroyton Quadrangles cover Red River Gorge. We suggest the following dayhikes:

Courthouse Rock via Trail 204. Courthouse Rock (CHR) is a massive rock formation at the north end of Auxier Ridge, near the west end of the National Recreation Area. From its trailhead lot, off Tunnel Ridge Road (TRR), the **Auxier Ridge Trail (204)** winds northward atop the ridge, passing Haystack Rock (HR) along the way. This relatively easy hike is 3 miles roundtrip; plan 2 hours for the hike.

Gray's Arch via Trail 205. From its trailhead lot on Tunnel Ridge Road (TRR), the **Gray's Arch Trail (205)** curves westward through open forest where it intersects the **Rough Trail (221)**. Turn right, staying atop the ridge for a short distance and then take a sharp turn to the left, as **Trail 205/221** descends through a deep ravine. Nearing Gray's Arch (GA), the trail curves back to the south where a side path leads down to the base of the span. Return via the same route, completing a 2.5 mile roundtrip hike.

Loop Hike 227-221-223. This 4 mile loop hike begins and ends at the Pinch-em Tight Trailhead on Tunnel Ridge Road (TRR) which services the **Sheltowee Trace Trail (STT)**, the **Pinch-em Tight Trail (223)** and the **Rush Ridge Trail (227)**. Hike eastward on the common entry to **Trails 223 and 227** and then angle left (northeast) on **Trail 227** which runs atop Rush Ridge for almost 1 mile. Turn right at the **Rough Trail (221)** intersection, descending into the Rush Branch valley and then climbing on to Pinch-em Tight Ridge. Pick up the **Pinch-em Tight Trail (223)** atop the ridge and follow it westward to the trailhead. Trail 223 is also a portion of the **Sheltowee Trace Trail** (see Chapter II).

Loop Hike 220-221-223-226. This 6 mile loop hike begins and ends at Koomer Ridge Campground; dayhiker parking is provided at the west end of the Campground Area. Pick up the **Koomer Ridge Trail (220)** and hike northeastward atop the ridge. Just past its junction with **Trail 226**, the **Koomer Ridge Trail** begins a long descent to Chimney Top Creek (CTC) where it intersects the **Rough Trail (221)**. Turn left on **Trail 221** (part of the

One of many vistas at Red River Gorge

Sheltowee Trace Trail) and prepare for a long, winding climb on to Pinch-em Tight Ridge. Atop the ridge, turn left on **Trail 223** and then left on the **Buck Trail (226)**. Follow the **Buck Trail** as it descends to the Right Fork of Chimney Top Creek and then climbs on to Koomer Ridge to intersect **Trail 220**. Turn right and hike back to the trailhead area.

 Rock Bridge Loop (207). This 1.5 mile loop trail begins and ends at the Rock Bridge Picnic Area at the east end of Rock Bridge Road (RBR). Once paved to retard erosion and improve access to Rock Bridge (RB) and Creation Falls (CF), the route is now a mix of paved and earthen sections. Hiking the loop clockwise, you will soon arrive at an overlook above the Swift Camp Creek (SCC) valley. A rather steep descent takes you down to the west bank of the stream, where the **Swift Creek Trail (219)** heads northward, along the creek. Turn right, staying on the **Rock Bridge Trail (207)** and you will soon reach the Bridge itself. The trail now turns westward, passing Creation Falls (CF) and climbs along a tributary of Swift Creek. Leaving the creek, **Trail 207** makes a steep ascent to the ridgetop, emerging from the forest at the Picnic Area.

 Rough Trail (221). By using two cars, or by arranging transportation, one can hike the entire 8.4 mile length of the **Rough Trail (221)**. Access to Red River Gorge's longest trail is via an east trailhead on KY 715 or at the west terminus, on KY 77 (see overview map). Hikers should keep in mind that the rugged terrain will make this route seem much longer than its official mileage; bring plenty of food and water, notify someone of your plans and expect to take at least 6 hours to complete the one-way trek.

155

50 NATURAL BRIDGE STATE RESORT PARK

Original Trail-Balanced Rock Loop
  Distance: 1.5 miles
  Terrain: hilly
  Walking time: 1 hour

Whittleton Arch
  Distance: 2 mi roundtrip
  Terrain: rolling; short hill
  Walking time: 1.5 hours

Rock Garden-Battleship Rock Loop
  Distance: 4 miles
  Terrain: hilly
  Walking time: 2.5 hours

Henson's Arch Trail
  Distance: .6 mi roundtrip
  Terrain: hilly
  Walking time: .5 hour

Sand Gap-Hoods Branch Loop
  Distance: 12 miles
  Terrain: hilly
  Walking time: 8 hours

Named for its famous sandstone arch that overlooks the Middle Fork of the Red River, **Natural Bridge State Resort Park** was donated to the State of Kentucky by the Louisville & Nashville Railroad in 1926, making it one of the four original Parks in Kentucky's fine State Park System. Its magnificent rock span is one of more than 150 natural bridges throughout the Red River Valley, a reflection of the region's geology. Resistant Pennsylvanian sandstone, overlying softer sediments of the Carboniferous Period, has been carved by water, wind and freeze-thaw erosion to create a wonderland of rock cliffs, ledges, natural bridges, rock towers and cascades.

While sections of the Park have been developed for the comfort and convenience of tourists, almost 1000 acres have been set aside as a State Nature Preserve, dedicated to the protection of native flora and fauna. Among the endangered species that inhabit the area are the Virginia big-eared bat and the small yellow lady's slipper. The Park's remote areas are reached by a fine network of hiking trails and a "skylift" transports those who cannot (or should not) attempt the climb to the Natural Bridge.

Directions: From the Mountain Parkway, southeast of Winchester, take the Slade Exit (Exit 33) and drive south on KY 11. The Park will be 2 miles ahead; proceed to parking areas as illustrated on the map. Most trails are best accessed from the large parking lot at the Gift Shop (GS), .5 miles south of the Lodge/Skylift entrance.

Routes: There are numerous potential dayhikes at Natural Bridge State Resort Park. We suggest the following routes:

Original Trail-Balanced Rock Loop. This first and easiest trail to the Park's Natural Bridge is known as the **Original Trail (1)**. This .75 mile trail (one way) begins on the paved drive that curves southward from the

156

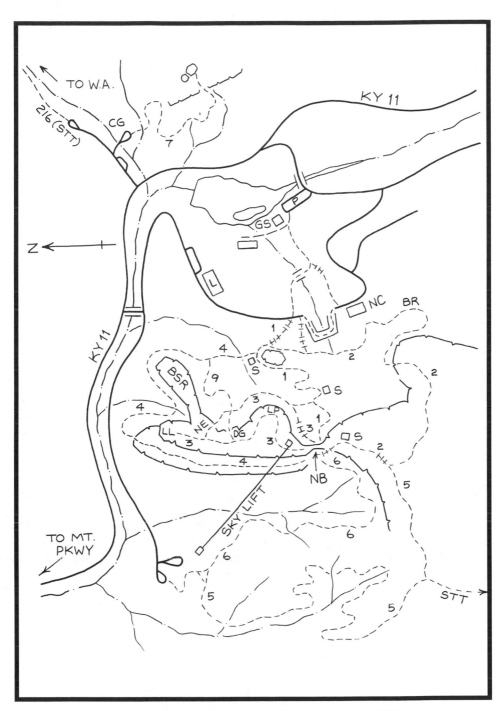

NATURAL BRIDGE STATE RESORT PARK

Lodge (L). While it does provide the easiest walk to the Bridge, this trail is **not easy**; unconditioned visitors, and those with a history of heart or lung disease, should consider riding the Skylift to view the Bridge. The loop described below yields a dayhike of 1.5 miles; plan at least 1 hour of walking time.

Hikers will first negotiate a series of stairs that lead up to a multi-trail intersection. Continue straight ahead, bypassing the cutoff to the **Rock Garden Trail (4)** and bearing left at the shelter (S). The **Original Trail** now curves to the south and ascends the ridge via a number of switchbacks. Bypass the **Battleship Rock Trail (3)**, just across from another shelter (S) and continue up to the Natural Bridge (NB).

Climb to the top of the Bridge from its west side and pick up the **Balanced Rock Trail (2)** south of the span. Leading further south, the trail forks; turn left, continuing along the **Balanced Rock Trail** and begin a winding descent back to the Lodge driveway (see map). Nearing the base of the ridge, the trail passes Balanced Rock (BR), a large block of Pennsylvanian sandstone.

Rock Garden-Battleship Rock Loop. This 4 mile loop also originates on the paved drive south of the Lodge (L). Hike up the first segment of the **Original Trail (1)** and then turn right at the shelter (S), heading northward on the **Rock Garden Trail (4)**. Bypass the **Salt Mine Trail (9)**, continuing along the **Rock Garden Trail** as it curves around Battleship Rock (BSR), passing giant slump blocks along the way. After crossing a stream, the trail leads to the north end of the ridge where it curves southward and climbs along the rock cliffs via a series of narrow stairways and catwalks.

Leading southward above the broad valley of Upper Hood's Branch, the **Rock Garden Trail** passes under the Skylift and soon arrives at the Natural Bridge (NB). Ascend to the top of the Bridge via a stairway on its west side and hike back across the span, picking up the **Battleship Rock Trail (3)**. This trail heads northward atop the ridge, passes the the Skylift and loops eastward to Lookout Point (LP). After taking in the view, continue along the **Battleship Rock Trail** to Lover's Leap (LL), the highest and northernmost overlook. Backtrack to either **Needle's Eye (NE)** or **Devil's Gulch (DG)** and descend from the ridgetop.

At the base of the cliffs, hike southward on the **Battleship Rock Trail (3)** and then descend to the Lodge driveway via the **Original Trail (1)**.

Sand Gap-Hood's Branch Loop. Adventurous and conditioned hikers may want to challenge themselves with this 12 mile dayhike which begins and ends at a picnic area near the base of the Skylift (see map). Climb onto the end of the ridge via a switchback and then bear right on to the **Sand Gap Trail (5)** which leads westward across the wooded hillside. Nearing Lower Hood's Branch, the trail turns upstream, paralleling the main creek and crossing its feeder streams via wooden bridges. Climbing higher to skirt a rhododendron thicket, the **Sand Gap Trail** continues southward into the upper reaches of Lower Hood's Branch which it eventually crosses.

*Sandstone cliffs along
the Rock Garden Trail*

The trail now turns northward above the west bank of the creek and parallels the stream for almost 2 miles. Angling to the west, the trail climbs on to the ridge and begins a long, nearly level excursion to the south end of the Natural Bridge (NB). Enroute, you will notice a cutoff to White's Branch Arch; this is where the **Sheltowee Trace Trail (STT)** exits southward from the Park.

From the west side of the Natural Bridge, pick up the **Hood's Branch Trail (6)** which curves around the highest reaches of Upper Hood's Branch, passing beneath rock cliffs and recessed caves. Turning northward along the west wall of the valley, this trail nears the creek at the site of an old homestead and then follows an old forest road to the trailhead area.

Whittleton Trail (216) to Whittleton Arch. The **Whittleton Trail**, which coincides with a segment of the **Sheltowee Trace Trail (STT)** is 2 miles in length, stretching from the Whittleton Campground (WCG) at Natural Bridge State Resort Park, to the south end of Tunnel Ridge Road (an entry point for the Red River Gorge National Recreation Area). The trail also provides access to Whittleton Arch (WA) which is reached via a side trail (see map). The hike from the Campground to the Arch is approximately 2 miles (roundtrip).

Henson's Arch Trail (7). This short (.3 mile) but steep trail also begins at the Whittleton Campground (see map). After ascending through a ravine, the trail loops southward above KY 11 where it passes through the cliff wall and ends at a sinkhole. Henson's Arch has eroded from the edge of the hole which can be entered by descending a ladder. Return via the same route, completing a roundtrip hike of .6 mile.

51 CENTRAL KENTUCKY WILDLIFE MANAGEMENT AREA

Combined Loop Hike
 Distance: 3 miles
 Terrain: rolling
 Walking time: 2 hours

The **Central Kentucky Wildlife Management Area,** just south of Kingston, offers a pleasant stroll through the rolling terrain of the Outer Bluegrass Region. Open meadows, cedar glades, riparian woodlands and thicket-lined streams characterize the preserve.

Wildlife is abundant here. White-tailed deer, red fox, skunks, raccoons and eastern cottontails are among the resident mammals. Meadowlarks, bobwhites, grassland sparrows and eastern bluebirds forage on the meadows while flickers, downy woodpeckers, northern cardinals and other songbirds scour the woodlands and thickets. Kestrels, red-tailed hawks and turkey vultures patrol the grasslands by day, replaced by great horned owls as dusk envelops the refuge. Mallards, muskrats, herons and migrant waterfowl may be spotted at the marsh-lined pond, a haven for frogs and painted turtles during the warmer months.

Directions: Take Exit #87 from I-75 and head east to U.S. 421. Turn right (south) on this highway and drive approximately 6 miles to Kingston. Proceed through town and watch for a county road that heads east from U.S. 421; this road is marked with a Wildlife Management Area sign. Drive 1.5 miles to the refuge entrance and park in the gravel lot near the pond (see map).

Route: The **Wildlife Area** is laced with a network of jeep trails and mowed paths, many of which are illustrated on the map. Obviously, a wide variety of potential day hikes can be achieved; we suggest the following 3 mile route.

Follow the jeep trail that leads eastward from the north side of the pond, descending toward a stream bed. After crossing this wooded drainage the path climbs along the edge of a hill where it intersects numerous side trails. Stay on the main path as it winds eastward across the grassland and crosses the stream once again.

The trail dips across a tributary and then leads along the north side of a meadow. Take the second path on your right which is bordered by two treelines; this path splits for a short distance, crosses the creek and eventually curves to the west. Continue to a point where two side trails parallel one another (see map) and hike northward across this meadow; turn left at the end of this path, descend to cross a stream and then turn right at the next intersection, following this creek-side route back to the central jeep trail.

Turn left (west) on the jeep trail and return to the parking area.

Open meadows and riparian woodlands characterize the preserve

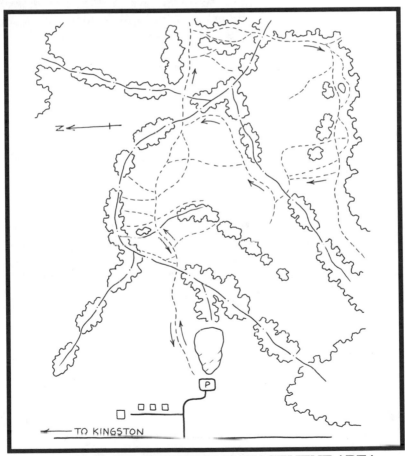

Z

TO KINGSTON

CENTRAL KY. WILDLIFE MANAGEMENT AREA

52 BEREA COLLEGE FOREST

Indian Fort Mountain
  Distance: 2.5 miles roundtrip
  Terrain: hilly
  Walking time: 2 hours

West Pinnacle
  Distance: 4 miles roundtrip
  Terrain: hilly
  Walking time: 2.5-3 hours

Buzzard Roost-Eagle Nest
  Distance: 4.5 miles roundtrip
  Terrain: hilly
  Walking time: 3 hours

East Pinnacle
  Distance: 3.5 miles roundtrip
  Terrain: hilly
  Walking time: 2.5 hours

Most dayhikers look for routes with three characteristics: well engineered trails, reasonable distances and scenic rewards for their effort. The trail network at **Berea College Forest** offers all three.

Located 3 miles east of the College, the Berea College Forest cloaks a truncated ridge at the western edge of the Appalachian Plateau. Rocky overlooks are spaced across the ridge, offering spectacular views of other Plateau "knobs" and of the Outer Bluegrass Region to the west.

Directions: From I-75, take Exit 76 and head east on KY 21. Drive 1.5 miles and bear right at the Boone Tavern Hotel, staying on KY 21. Another 3.1 miles bring you to a large parking area, on your left, which services the Indian Fort Amphitheater and the Berea College Forest trails.

Routes: There are over 19 miles of hiking trails within the Forest. We suggest the following routes:

Indian Fort Mountain. Enter the forest on the common access path that leads northward from the parking lot, passes the Amphitheater (A) and climbs along a stream. Bypass the cutoff to East Pinnacle, on your right, and continue northward. Cross through a trail intersection and begin to climb more steeply, passing a natural spring (S) before reaching the top of the ridge. Head across to the Devil's Kitchen (DK), a large, recessed cave on the north side of the ridge, and then follow the trail that loops along the edge of Indian Fort Mountain (IFM). Magnificent overlooks are spaced along the west side of this spur ridge. After completing the loop, return to the parking lot via your entry route (see map), for a total hike of 2.5 miles.

West Pinnacle. A 4 mile roundtrip hike will take you to the west end of the Forest's high plateau. Climb to the ridgetop on the central, entry trail, as described for Indian Fort Mountain (above). Once atop the ridge, turn left and hike westward along the narrow spine that leads out to the West Pinnacle (WP;see map). Return to your car via the same route.

Buzzard Roost-Eagle Nest. This 4.5 mile route takes you to both the Buzzard Roost(BR) and Eagle Nest(EN) Overlooks, along the northeast edge of the ridge. Follow the entry trail past the Amphitheater (A) and natural spring (S). Once atop the ridge, turn right and proceed to the trail

*A view from
Indian Fort Mt.*

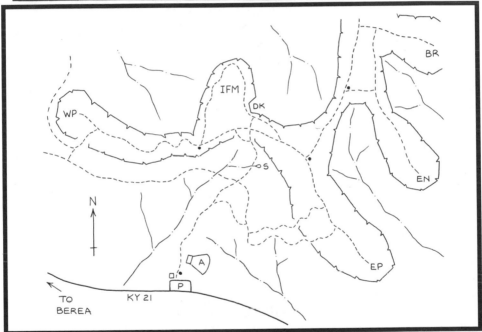

BEREA COLLEGE FOREST

intersection where a sign directs you northward to Buzzard Roost and Eagle
Nest. After hiking to both of these overlooks, as illustrated on the map,
return to the lot via your entry route.

   East Pinnacle. Enter the forest along the common entry path, pass
the Amphitheater (A) and take the first trail on your right. Turn right at the
next intersection and climb on to the ridge via one of two trails that make a
steep ascent to the east (see map). Once atop the ridge, turn right and hike
out to the East Pinnacle Overlook (EP). Return via the same route, completing a roundtrip hike of 3.5 miles.

53 TURKEY FOOT RECREATION AREA

KY 89 to Recreation Area
   Distance: 3.5 miles (7 miles roundtrip)
   Terrain: hilly
   Walking time: 2.5 hours (5 hours roundtrip)

A section of the **Sheltowee Trace Trail** (see Chapter II) crosses Ky 89 just south of Foxton, Kentucky, and descends eastward to the **Turkey Foot Recreation Area** on the War Branch of Station Camp Creek. This 3.5 mile route (7 miles roundtrip) passes a scenic, rock-walled gorge, skirts a clear-cut area and descends through a rich forest of hardwood and pine.

Parking is available at either end of this trail section and visitors with two cars can limit their excursion to the 3.5 mile, one-way distance. Those planning to hike the entire roundtrip distance may want to park at the **Recreation Area** (thereby completing the uphill portion first).

Directions: From McKee, on U.S. 421, head north on Ky 89. Drive 4.5 miles and turn right; park near the utility station just east of Ky 89.

The turnoff to **Turkey Foot Recreation Area** is on the east side of Ky 89, approximately 3 miles north of McKee. This road descends northeastward to the **Recreation Area** which stretches along the west bank of the War Branch of Station Camp Creek. The latter is a tributary of the Kentucky River.

Route: From the utility station on Ky 89, hike eastward on the **Sheltowee Trace Trail (STT)** which parallels a roadway and then curves northward, passing near the edge of a scenic, rock-walled gorge. Angling to the southwest, the trail crosses the road, parallels it once again and then turns southward along the edge of a clear-cut area (CC). While clearcuts are all-too-common across the Appalachian Plateau, they can be excellent sites for wildlife watching; deer browse in these artificial clearings from dusk to dawn and such disrupted woodlands provide hunting grounds for hawks, owls, coyotes and fox. White pine is slowly invading the clearcut which, if left undisturbed, will eventually succumb to the surrounding forest.

Entering the woods, the trail curves eastward to skirt a drainage and begins a long, gradual descent to the **Turkey Foot Recreation Area**. Hikers will notice that the soil is sandy in this region, having eroded from Carboniferous sandstone that caps the ridges of the Appalachian Plateau. Rhododendron is common throughout the forest and, deep within the valley, stands of eastern hemlock rise along the stream, adding to the scenic beauty of this peaceful retreat.

The **Sheltowee Trace Trail** emerges from the forest at the **Recreation Area** and turns northward along the War Branch of Station Camp Creek. Those

*Entering the
clear-cut*

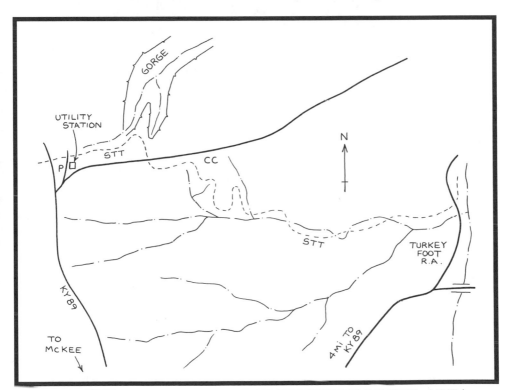

THE SHELTOWEE TRACE NEAR TURKEY FOOT REC. AREA

planning a roundtrip hike may want to enjoy a picnic lunch along the creek
before returning to KY 89 via the same route.

54 BUCKHORN LAKE STATE RESORT PARK

Combined Loop Hike
 Distance: 2.5 miles
 Terrain: hilly
 Walking time: 1.5-2.0 hrs.

Stretching above the north shore of Buckhorn Lake, **Buckhorn Lake State Resort Park** is the only State Park in Kentucky that is named for a local community (Buckhorn, Kentucky, is .5 mile downstream). The 1200 acre Lake was created by damming the Middle Fork of the Kentucky River, a U.S. Army Corps of Engineers project, completed in August, 1960.

Two hiking trails lead across a wooded ridge, north and east of the Lodge, offering a combined hike of 2.5 miles.

Directions: From Hazard, head north on KY 15. Drive 9 miles, turn left (west) on KY 28 and proceed another 10 miles to KY 1833. Follow this road to the Park (approximately 4 miles).

Route: A common entry path for the **Leatherwood Trail (LWT)** and **Moonshiner's Hollow Trail (MHT)** climbs eastward from the Park road, just northeast of the Lodge (see map). At the trail junction, turn left on the **Leatherwood Trail** which crosses a footbridge and then assaults the hill via a long stairway. Hike clockwise along the loop which yields views of the lake before turning back near a powerline swath. Complete the trail loop and descend back to the entry path.

Turn left on to the **Moonshiner's Hollow Trail** for a long, undulating route along the valley wall. This is a self-guided nature trail; markers are spaced along the path and an interpretive brochure is available at the Park Lodge. The trail passes behind a group of cottages and then curves to the northeast, crossing several drainages. Beyond these stream beds, the trail levels out and enters an area of mature, deciduous forest. Wildflowers carpet the forest in April, completing their cycle before the woodland's canopy closes out the sun.

Nearing the east end of the loop, the **Moonshiner's Hollow Trail** turns southward and descends along a creek. After crossing the stream, the trail curves to the east, fords another drainage via a footbridge and then climbs to the Park road. Turn right and follow the roadway back to the Lodge (see map).

166

*The Moonshiner's
Hollow Trail*

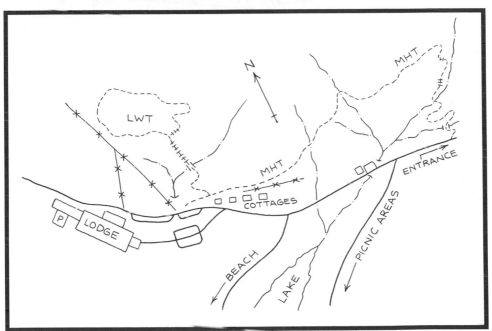

THE LEATHERWOOD & MOONSHINER'S HOLLOW TRAILS

55 PAINTSVILLE LAKE

Kiwanis Nature Trail
Distance: 2 miles (from lot)
Terrain: rolling
Walking time: 1.5 hrs.

East Shore Hikes
Distance: hikes of 3.0-4.6 miles
Terrain: rolling
Walking time: hikes of 2-3 hrs.

Paintsville Lake, a few miles northwest of Paintsville, Kentucky, is a popular destination for boaters and fishermen. Constructed by the U.S. Army Corps of Engineers for flood control and recreation, the Lake covers almost 1200 acres and winds for 18 miles through Johnson and Morgan Counties. **Paintsville Lake State Park**, just north of the dam, is a day-use area with picnic grounds and a privately-owned marina.

The **Kiwanis Nature Trail**, a 1.25 mile, graveled path, winds along the Lake's south shore and through a variety of natural habitats. Designated a National Recreation Trail, this path was constructed by the local Kiwanis Club in cooperation with the U.S. Army Corps of Engineers. Hikers may also want to explore a network of gravel roads along the eastern shore of Paintsville Lake (described below).

Directions: From U.S. 23 on the north side of Paintsville, turn west on U.S. 460. Proceed .5 mile and turn right on KY 40W. Drive another 1.6 miles and turn right on KY 2275; the Dam area will be .6 mile ahead.

To reach the gravel roads east of the Lake, turn north from KY 40 on to KY 172 (see overview map). Proceed 3.2 miles to Volga and turn left on Stonecoal Branch Road. The lakeshore will be 2.7 miles ahead.

Routes: Kiwanis Nature Trail. Park in the lot at the east end of the dam and hike westward along the road to the Kiwanis Nature Trail sign, on the right side of the road (see map). The 1.25 mile, graveled trail leads northwestward above the south shore of Paintsville Lake and then turns to the south along an inlet. After passing the spillway, the trail climbs along a stream bed and then enters a wooded meadow where deer and wild turkeys may be encountered. At the east end of the meadow, the trail turns northward along a gravel road, crosses the spillway once again and then climbs to the Park road through the Mountain Homeplace Historic Area. Return to your car via the roadway, completing a total hike of 2.0 miles.

East Shore Hikes. The graveled roads that run along the eastern shore of Paintsville Lake can be used for a variety of dayhikes. The terrain is gently rolling and views of the Lake are spaced along the way. We suggest the following routes:

> **Stonecoal Branch (SCB) to Joe's Creek Road (JCR) - 4.6 miles r.trip**
> **Joe's Creek Road (JCR) to Road's north end - 2.8 miles roundtrip**
> **Open Fork Road - 3 miles roundtrip from KY 172 to gate near boat ramp area**

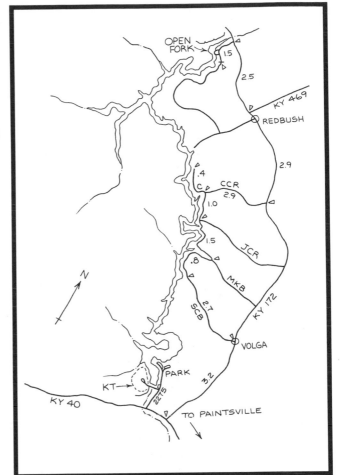

PAINTSVILLE LAKE & VICINITY

OPEN FORK
1.5
2.5
KY 469
REDBUSH
2.9
.4
C
CCR
2.9
1.0
1.5
JCR
.8
MKB
2.7
SCB
KY 172
VOLGA
N
3.2
PARK
KT
2275
KY 40
TO PAINTSVILLE

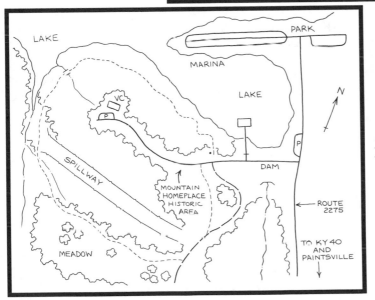

KIWANIS NATURE TRAIL

LAKE
PARK
MARINA
LAKE
N
VC
P
P
SPILLWAY
DAM
ROUTE 2275
MOUNTAIN HOMEPLACE HISTORIC AREA
TO KY 40 AND PAINTSVILLE
MEADOW

56 JENNY WILEY STATE RESORT PARK

Lakeshore Trail
  Distance: 2.6 mile loop
  Terrain: hilly
  Walking time: 2 hours

Moss Ridge Trail
  Distance: 1.3 miles
  Terrain: hilly
  Walking time: 1 hour

Jenny Wiley Trail (Trailhead to CG)
  Distance: 6 miles roundtrip
  Terrain: hilly
  Walking time: 4 hours

Dedicated in 1962, **Jenny Wiley State Resort Park** honors the memory of Virginia Sellards "Jenny" Wiley, a pioneer woman who was captured by the Shawnee and Cherokee Indians in 1789. Having witnessed the massacre of her brother and children, Jenny remained a hostage for six months, finally escaping near the Big Sandy River. She and her husband resettled in the Big Sandy Valley where she died and was buried in 1831.

The State Resort Park stretches along the south shore of Dewey Lake, an 1100 acre reservoir completed in 1951. Two hiking trails originate at the Lodge and the Park is the southern terminus of the **Jenny Wiley Trail**, a 163 mile route that winds northward to South Portsmouth, on the Ohio River (see Chapter II). Four miles of the **Trail**, which follows the general path of Jenny and her captors, lie within the State Resort Park.

Directions: The west entrance to the Park is via KY 3 which cuts east from U.S. 23, 5.5 miles north of Prestonsburg (8.5 miles south of Paintsville). Proceed to parking areas as shown on the map.

Routes: Lakeshore Trail (LST). A 2.6 mile hike is achieved by hiking eastward along the south shore of Dewey Lake and then returning to the Lodge area via the Park roadway. Descend a long flight of stairs that lead down to the Marina from the Lodge (see map). Turn right on the Marina drive and pick up the **Lakeshore Trail** which undulates eastward along the shoreline. Bypass the shortcut path and continue to the end of the loop which curves southward and climbs to the Park road. Hike back to the Lodge area along this roadway, completing a 2.6 mile loop.

Moss Ridge Trail (MRT). This 1.3 mile loop begins just south of the Lodge (see map). After climbing into the forest, the trail forks; continue straight ahead to the next trail intersection where a spur trail descends to the Park's Amphitheater (A). Stay on the **Moss Ridge Trail** for an elongated, winding loop across the ridge. Once back at the entry path, turn right and exit to the roadway.

Jenny Wiley Trail (JWT). A three mile section of the **Jenny Wiley Trail** leads from its southern trailhead, near the Marina, to the Park's Campground (CG). The trail climbs on to a ridge via several switchbacks

A scene along the Lakeshore Trail

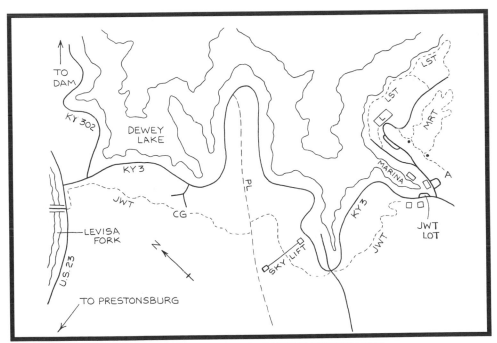

JENNY WILEY STATE RESORT PARK

and heads westward near its crest. After descending to cross a roadway, the trail curves northward, passes under the Skylift and then climbs on to a low ridge where it intersects a pipeline swath (PL). The route jogs left along this swath and then turns northward once again, descending to the campground area. Return to the Marina via the same route, completing a roundtrip hike of 6 miles.

171

Boone Trace Trail
 Distance: 2.3 miles
 Terrain: rolling; one stairway
 Walking time: 1.5 hours

Frazier Knob Trail
 Distance: 2.2 miles
 Terrain: hilly
 Walking time: 2 hours

Wilderness Road Trail
 Distance: 1 mile loop
 Terrain: rolling
 Walking time: .75 hour

Named for the first judge in Laurel County and for the famous pioneer trail of eastern Kentucky, **Levi Jackson Wilderness Road State Park** offers an attractive mix of natural beauty and human history. The Park's Mountain Life Museum (M) reproduces a 19th Century pioneer settlement and McHargue's Mill, on the banks of the Little Laurel River, is a restored grist mill, renowned for its large collection of millstones.

Nine miles of hiking trails provide access to the Park's natural areas; the three primary trails are described below.

Directions: From I-75, take Exit 38 and head east on KY 192. Drive 1.8 miles and turn right (south) on U.S. 25. Proceed 1.5 miles and turn left (east) on Ky 1006. The Park will be .5 mile ahead.

Routes: Boone Trace Trail (BT). This 2.3 mile trail begins just south of McHargue's Mill, climbing a hillside via a stairway and switchback. Following the route of a famous pioneer trail, the path angles to the southeast, passes a campground, winds through a parcel of forest and then crosses a Park road. After curving past the Park Office, the trail emerges from the woods at the main campground, crossing its entry road. Just beyond this road, the path forks; take either route and begin a long loop hike, skirting the Park's pool and maintenance area. After completing this loop, return to the Mill via your entry route.

Frazier Knob Trail (FKT). This 2.2 mile trail begins at the Stable (S) parking lot, descends across a drainage and then leads eastward along the south edge of the County Fairgrounds. Bypass side trails to the south, eventually crossing a power line swath and entering the ridgetop forest. Before turning north toward Frazier Knob (F), hike up to an overlook (V) which yields a broad view to the east (see map).

The **Frazier Knob Trail** undulates to the north, crossing two stream beds, and emerges from the forest at a roadside parking lot. Jog to the left to pick up the trail on the north side of the road (see map); the path climbs steeply and then levels out atop a ridge, using part of an old jeep road before its final

A forest view from Frazier Knob

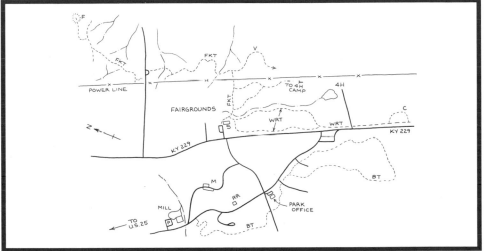

LEVI JACKSON WILDERNESS ROAD STATE PARK

ascent to Frazier Knob. This sandstone outcropping, the highest point in the State Park, yields a panoramic view during the "leafless" months of the year. After rest and nourishment atop the Knob, return to your car via the same route.

Wilderness Road Trail (WRT). This National Recreation Trail follows the route of the "Wilderness Road" which led early pioneers from the Cumberland Gap to the Ohio River Valley. The trail now parallels Ky 229 within the park; a side loop south of the 4-H Camp driveway leads to the Jackson Family Cemetery (C) while, north of the driveway, the trail makes a 1 mile loop through the oak-hickory forest. Access to either section of the trail is best achieved from the pool parking lot, just west of Ky 229. Be advised that portions of the trail loop were overgrown and difficult to follow at the time of our visit in 1993.

58 REDBIRD CREST TRAIL

Distance: Dayhikes up to 15 miles
Terrain: hilly
Walking time: Dayhikes up to 10 hours

Established as the "Cumberland National Forest" in 1937, the **Daniel Boone National Forest** (renamed in 1966) now covers over 670,000 acres across the Appalachian Plateau of eastern Kentucky. While the Forest's primary section stretches along the western edge of the Plateau, from the Big South Fork to the highlands north of Morehead, its **Redbird Purchase Unit** encompasses the upper watersheds of the Middle and South Forks of the Kentucky River.

Within the Redbird Purchase Unit is the **Redbird Crest Trail**, a 65 mile loop trail that circles the Redbird River Valley, south of the Daniel Boone Parkway. **"Redbird"** was a chief of the Cherokee Indian Tribe whose domain once stretched from southeastern Kentucky to the Great Smokey Mountains of Tennessee.

Directions: From the Daniel Boone Parkway, take Exit 34 and head south on KY 66. The Peabody Redbird Ranger Station (R) will be approximately 3 miles ahead, on your right. There is ample parking at the Station and this is certainly the most convenient and safe access point to the Redbird Crest Trail. Another recommended access point is off the east side of KY 66, 14 miles south of the Ranger Station; a gravel road climbs up from KY 66, 1.7 miles south of the KY 406 junction, and ends at an old mine parking lot (M).

Routes: The entire 65 mile loop is, obviously, a bit long for a dayhike. Furthermore, Darrell Pennington, a recreation technician for the U.S. Forest Service, informed us that some sections of the Trail, especially along its eastern rim, are devoid of safe parking areas; indeed he reported that there is limited access within the entire Redbird Wildlife Managment Area (WMA). In addition, the 5 mile stretch north of KY 406 is currently being re-routed.

We thus suggest the following dayhikes:

Ranger Station (R) to Big Double Creek Campground (CG). This 4 mile hike (8 miles roundtrip) begins at the Peabody Redbird Ranger Station. Walk eastward along KY 66 and pick up the Redbird Crest Trail at the junction of Big Double Creek Road (Forest Road 1501). The trail climbs steadily toward the southeast, ascending a forested ridge. Leveling out atop the ridge, the trail winds toward the south. After hiking almost 2 miles along the crest, watch for a side trail that descends toward an old gas well (G). Descend via this path, turn left on the roadway and hike another .5 mile to the Campground (CG). After rest and nourishment at this creekside area, return to the Ranger Station via the same route.

Old Mine Lot (M) Access. From this parking area off the east side

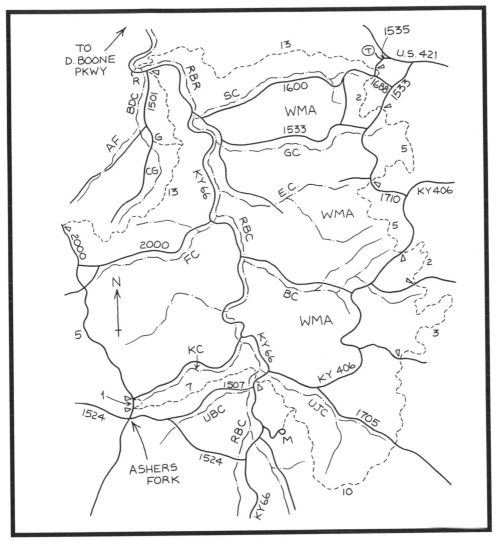

REDBIRD CREST TRAIL

of KY 66 (see Directions above), a path climbs northeastward to the Redbird Crest Trail. Turning either direction, one can hike 2-3 miles atop the ridge before encountering any steep trail sections. Return via the same route, completing a roundtrip hike of 5-7 miles.

Lucinda Tower (T) to the Ranger Station (R). By arranging transportation, one can access the Forest at the old Lucinda fire tower off U.S. 421 west of Hyden, Kentucky. Hike southward along Forest Road 1535 to the Redbird Crest Trail crossing (almost 2 miles) and turn right (west) on the Trail. Most of the 13 mile route back to the Ranger Station stays near the crest of a ridge but numerous "saddles" and stream crossings are encountered along the way. Plan at least 10 hours for this strenuous, one-way hike.

59 BAD BRANCH STATE NATURE PRESERVE

Hike to Bad Branch Falls
   Distance: 2.5 miles roundtrip
   Terrain: hilly; steep areas
   Walking time: 1.5-2.0 hours

Hike to the High Rock Crest
   Distance: 7 miles roundtrip
   Terrain: hilly; steep areas
   Walking time: 5.5 hours

For a good hike, head to **Bad Branch**. This scenic **State Nature Preserve** spreads across the south face of Pine Mountain, rising 1000 feet above the Poor Fork of the Cumberland River. Drained by Bad Branch Creek and its tributaries, the rugged preserve is accessed by a 7.4 mile network of trails, including a short but steep path to Bad Branch Falls, a 60-foot cascade.

Encompassing 1640 acres, the refuge is protected by adjacent holdings of The Nature Conservancy and the Kentucky State Nature Preserve Commission. A rich hemlock-mixed mesophytic forest cloaks most of the preserve which harbors a number of rare and endangered species; among these are Fraser's sedge, painted trillium, matricary grapefern and the rose pogonia orchid. Kentucky's only known breeding pair of ravens nest on the high sandstone cliffs and Bad Branch Creek, added to the State Wild and Scenic River System in 1986, is inhabited by the endemic arrow darter.

Directions: From Whitesburg, head southwest on U.S. 119, crossing Pine Mountain. Seven miles from Whitesburg, turn left (east) on KY 932 and proceed 1.7 miles to the Nature Preserve, on your left. Dogs are not permitted in the Preserve.

Routes: The Nature Preserve's entry trail leads northward from the parking lot, crossing and then recrossing Bad Branch Creek. Following the Creek upstream, you will reach the cutoff to **Bad Branch Falls** within one mile. Bear right, descending to cross a tributary of Bad Branch, and then begin a winding ascent to the magnificent Falls (see map). Return to the parking area via the same route, completing a roundtrip hike of 2.5 miles.

Energetic and conditioned hikers may want to press on to the **High Rock** area atop Pine Mountain. To do so, turn right at the main trail junction and continue northward along a major tributary of Bad Branch (see map). The trail eventually crosses this stream and follows one of its forks toward the northeast. After crossing a spur ridge of the Mountain's backbone, the trail dips to a streamside junction where a loop trail follows the upper arms of Bad Branch Creek. Turn left and climb along the West Fork to the crest of Pine Mountain.

The trail turns northeastward atop the ridge, crossing the **High Rock** area. The terrain plummets steeply to the north of the trail's route and spectacular views reward your effort. Further along the crest, the trail angles southward and descends along the East Fork of Bad Branch Creek. A four hundred foot descent over 1.5 miles brings you to the junction of the East and West Forks; the loop trail crosses Bad Branch Creek at this junction and

Bad Branch Falls

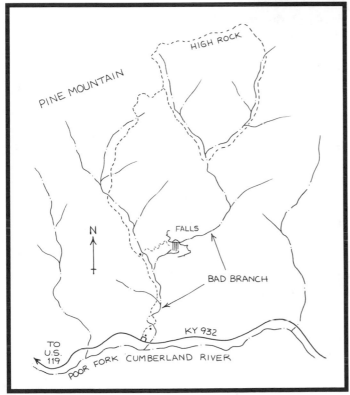

**BAD BRANCH
STATE NATURE
PRESERVE**

climbs along the West Fork to meet the main trail which leads back to the parking area (see map).

Those who hike the entire trail system, including the side trip to the Falls, will cover 7.4 miles; plan at least 5.5-6.0 hours to complete this strenuous journey.

60 KINGDOM COME STATE PARK

Distance: Dayhikes of 2.25 to 3.3 miles
Terrain: hilly
Walking time: Dayhikes of 1.5 to 2.0 hours

Perched atop Pine Mountain at an elevation of nearly 2800 feet, **Kingdom Come** is the highest **State Park** in Kentucky. Its numerous overlooks yield spectacular views across the Appalachian Plateau to the north and along the Cumberland Valley to the south.

The Park's 1027 acres, graced by a 3.5 acre lake and centered on a giant outcropping of sandstone (Raven Rock), are accessed by a network of 13 hiking trails, none of which is more than a mile in length. However, by combining these routes, one can achieve a variety of dayhikes in the 2-3 mile range. Furthermore, the **Little Shepherd Trail (LST)** , a 38-mile route that follows the crest of Pine Mountain through Harlan and Letcher Counties, cuts through the State Park; see Chapter II for more information on this trail. Hikers should be aware that an increasing number of black bears have been observed at the Park; make some noise along the trail to warn them of your presence and be especially cautious in shrubby areas.

Directions: Kingdom Come State Park is off KY 1254 on the east side of Cumberland, Kentucky, 23 miles WSW of Whitesburg (via U.S. 119). Wind up the Park's entry road for 1.5 miles and park in the lot on the south shore of the Lake (see map).

Routes: Parking areas and trailheads are spaced along the Park roads (see map); most of the dayhikes that we recommend originate at the lot on the Lake's southern shore.

Hikes to Raven Rock. Raven Rock (RR), a giant sandstone outcropping and the most striking natural feature at the Park, can be reached via several routes:

Lake Trail (LK)-Ivy Trail-Raven Rock Trail (RRT). This route yields a roundtrip hike of 2.25 miles. Opening a broad swath on the south face of Pine Mountain, Raven Rock yields magnificent views across the Cumberland River Valley. When venturing on to the Rock, be advised that its steep pitch and weathered surface make for treacherous footing.

Log Rock Trail (LRT)-Park Road-Ground Hog Trail (GT). This route to Raven Rock begins at the Gazebo Overlook (G) southeast of the Lake (see map). The Log Rock Trail (LRT) follows the rim of a deep gorge as it leads northeastward to the Log Rock Overlook (LR). Continue along the trail to the Park Road and climb northward along the roadway to the Ground Hog Trail (GT). This path leads westward to Raven Rock (RR). Return to the lakeside parking lot via the same route, completing a round-trip hike of 2.5 miles

Lake Trail (LK)-Laurel Trail (LT)-Powerline Trail (PL)- Raven Rock Trail (RRT). This route leads directly north to the base of Raven

Raven Rock

KINGDOM COME STATE PARK

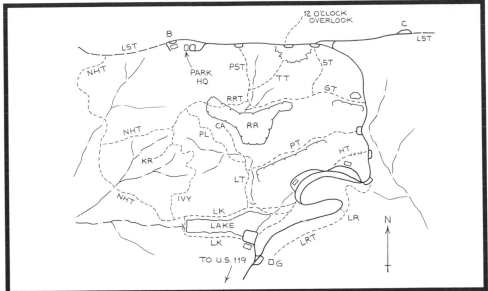

Rock and then skirts its western edge by climbing along a powerline swath. The roundtrip distance totals 2.25 miles. Plan a short side trip to the Cave Amphitheater (CA) along the way.

Park Loop. A 3.3 mile loop hike can be achieved by the following route. From the Lake parking lot, hike westward on the **Lake Trail (LK)** and then pick up the **Nature Haven Trail (NHT)** west of the dam. This trail winds upward and northward for almost 1 mile and intersects the **Little Shepherd Trail** atop the ridge. Hike eastward on this trail, stop by the Bullock Overlook (B) and continue along the Park road to the **Possum Trail (PST)**. Descend to Raven Rock (RR), take in the view and then head east on the **Ground Hog Trail (GHT)**. Follow this trail to the Park road, turn right along the roadway and then right again on the **Pine Trail (PT)** which descends to the base of Raven Rock. Turn left (south) on the **Laurel Trail (LT)** and return to the Lake area.

Creech Overlook. Park at the trailhead lot for the **Saltess Trail (ST)** and hike eastward on a paved section of the hike the **Little ShepherdTrail (LST)** to the Creech Overlook (C). Return via the same route for a 1.6 mile hike.

179

Hemlock Garden Trail
Distance: 1 mile loop
Terrain: hilly
Walking time: .75 hour

Honeymoon Falls Trail
Distance: 1.5 mile loop
Terrain: hilly
Walking time: 1.25 hours

Living Stairway-Fern Garden
Distance: 1.5 mile
Terrain: hilly
Walking time: 1.25 hours

Lost Trail-Living Stairway
Distance: 1.0 mile
Terrain: hilly
Walking time: .75 hour

Chained Rock Trail
Distance: 1 mile roundtrip
Terrain: hilly
Walking time: 1 hour

Rock Hotel Trail
Distance: 2 miles roundtrip
Terrain: hilly
Walking time: 1.75 hours

Laurel Cove Trail
Distance: 3.5 miles roundtrip
Terrain: hilly
Walking time: 2.75 hours

Azalea Trail
Distance: .5 mile loop
Terrain: hilly
Walking time: .5 hour

Kentucky Ridge Tower
Distance: 3 miles roundtrip
Terrain: rolling
Walking time: 2 hours

Established in 1924, **Pine Mountain State Resort Park** is the oldest State Park in Kentucky; it is also one of the most beautiful. Stretching across the backbone of Kentucky Ridge State Forest, the Park harbors a fine network of hiking trails. Spectacular vistas, hidden waterfalls, luxurient woodlands and unique rock formations reward the "off-road" explorer.

One of the Park's more interesting features is **Laurel Cove**, a natural forest cove which has been transformed into a 3000 seat amphitheater, the site of the annual Mountain Laurel Festival. Timed to coincide with the blooming of this native shrub, the Festival is held during the last weekend in May.

Directions: From I-75, take Exit 29 and head southeast on U.S. 25E. Drive approximately 33 miles to Pineville, Kentucky. Continue through town, heading south toward Middlesboro; the Park entrances will be on the west side of U.S. 25E, 1-1.5 mile south of Pineville (see overview map).

A view to the south from Chained Rock

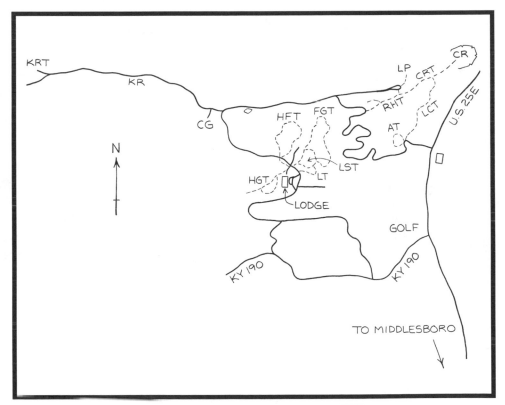

PINE MOUNTAIN STATE RESORT PARK
(OVERVIEW MAP)

Routes: A fine collection of hiking trails provides access to the scenic backcountry of **Pine Mountain State Resort Park**. We suggest the following dayhikes:

Kentucky Ridge Tower (KRT). A jeep road (KR) heads westward and then southwestward from the State Park Campground (CG), running atop the crest of Pine Mountain and into the Kentucky Ridge State Forest (see overview map, page 181). By parking near the Campground entrance, one can hike along this road to the site of the old Kentucky Ridge fire tower (KRT), approximately 1.5 miles from the Park boundary. Broad views extend to either side of the ridge, especially during the late fall and winter months. Return via the same route for a total hike of 3 miles.

Hemlock Garden Trail (HGT). This 1 mile hike begins along a service road just north of the Lodge (L). After walking a short distance you will reach a fork in the trail; bear right (straight ahead) and cross the stream via a foot bridge. This stream has carved a deep ravine on the south face of Pine Mountain, creating a cool, moist environment for the numerous hemlocks that dominate the woodland. American beech, tuliptrees and white oaks are also common here.

Continue out to Inspiration Point (IP) which overlooks a rhododendron thicket (see map, next page) and then return to the main loop, soon passing a shelter house (S) which was built by the Civilian Conservation Corps during the 1930s. After crossing and recrossing the stream, the trail begins a gradual ascent back to the Lodge. Large boulders rest within and near the stream, having broken from the cliffs along the east wall of the ravine; a side trail loops back across the creek, passing through "Fat Man's Squeeze" (FMS). A second side trail provides an alternate route back to the Lodge and takes you up to the Garden View Overlook (GV) for a pleasing vista across the rich, hemlock forest.

Honeymoon Falls Trail (HFT). This 1.5 mile hike also begins along the service road just north of the Lodge (L). After passing between two boulders, the trail leads westward above a drainage and then turns to the north and climbs to the Park road. Turn left for a short walk along the roadway and pick up the trail at a small parking lot (see map, next page). The path skirts an old reservoir and then winds along its feeder stream, crossing and recrossing the creek several times. Eastern hemlocks and rhododendrons are common in this moist woodland.

The trail soon arrives at the base of Honeymoon Falls, which plummets 25 feet from the sandstone bluffs; a second waterfall can be seen on the west wall of the ravine (see map). After climbing toward the northeast, the trail crosses the stream once again, loops through a boulder field and then begins a long, winding descent back to the Park road. Curving westward along a creek, the trail exits the forest at a picnic area parking lot.

Cross the road, pick up the entry path and return to the Lodge area.

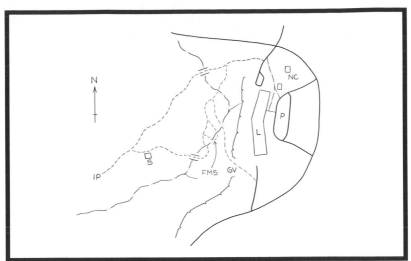

HEMLOCK GARDEN TRAIL

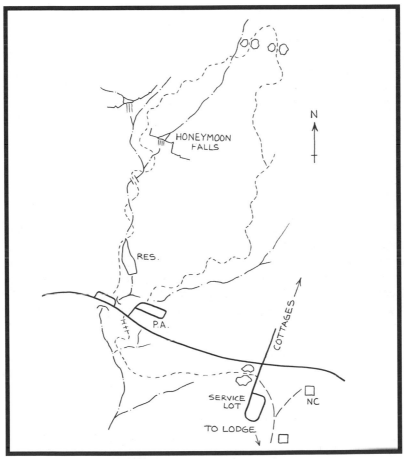

HONEYMOON FALLS TRAIL

Living Stairway-Fern Garden Loop. This 1.5 mile loop utilizes both the **Living Stairway Trail (LST)** and the **Fern Garden Trail (FGT)**. The hike begins along the Park road north of the Lodge and just east of the Cottage access road (see map). After descending from the road and crossing a creek, bear right at the fork in the path, re-crossing the stream and following the east arm of the **Living Stairway Trail**. This trail soon climbs on to a natural patio of sandstone which yields a fine view to the south. Wild blueberries will be found along the borders of this rocky overlook.

Turning northward, the trail follows the edge of a deep gorge and intersects the **Fern Garden Trail** at the **"Living Stairway (LS),"** a tuliptree (yellow poplar) that has somehow survived its use as a footpath. A man-made stairway parallels the old tree, descending into the rock-walled ravine and crossing the stream that carved it. The trail turns southward along the creek, passing beneath sandstone bluffs, and then angles to the left, climbing the east wall of the gorge. A winding route leads to the upper reaches of this forested valley, passing boulders and rock outcroppings along the way.

The **Fern Garden (FG)**, a dense growth of cinnamon and royal ferns, lies in a moist ravine near the top of the slope; sweet gum trees are also common in this area. The trail departs the garden and begins a long, gradual descent to the south. Nearing the cottages, you will intersect the **Living Stairway Trail**; bear right (straight ahead), following the stream to the Park road (see map).

Lost Trail-Living Stairway Trail Loop. A short (1 mile) but moderately strenuous hike can be achieved by combining the **Lost Trail (LT)** with a section of the **Living Stairway Trail (LST)**. Pick up the **Lost Trail** along the Park road, a short distance northeast of the Lodge (see map). This trail descends along a steep ravine, passing several rock formations along the way; the remnants of an old moonshiner's still can be seen in one of the recessed caves. Turning northward, the trail skirts the edge of a sandstone outcropping before climbing atop another. More winding and climbing brings you to the eastern edge of a large rock exposure which yields a broad view to the south. Hike westward across this slab and pick up the **Living Stairway Trail**; turn left on this path for a short walk back to the Park road (see map). Return to the Lodge via the service road and a paved walkway.

184

The Fern Garden

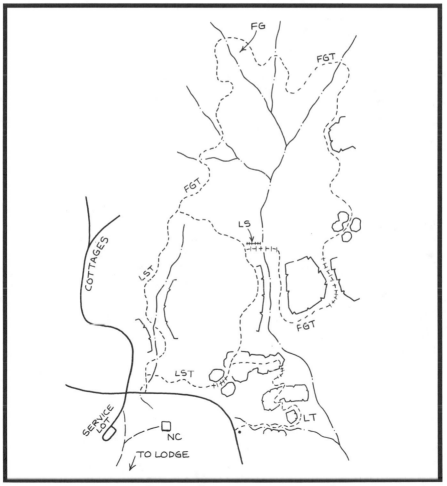

LIVING STAIRWAY-FERN GARDEN-LOST TRAIL

185

Chained Rock Trail (CRT). This .5 mile trail (1 mile roundtrip), begins at a ridgetop parking lot near the northern boundary of the Park (see map). Before setting out on the trail, follow a short path to **Lookout Point (LP)** for a sweeping view of the Cumberland Valley.

The **Chained Rock Trail** descends a stairway and then angles to the east for an undulating course to the **"Chained Rock (CR),"** a large boulder that was anchored to the rock cliff in 1933 to protect the town of Pineville, below. From this open area, visitors enjoy a panoramic view of this historic and scenic region; the Cumberland River Valley extends northwestward from Pineville and the rugged terrain of Kentucky Ridge State Forest dominates the view to the south. On a clear day, the high spine of Cumberland Mountain, 12 miles distant, can be seen to the SSE.

After taking in the view, return to the parking area via the same route.

Rock Hotel Trail (RHT). This 1 mile trail (2 miles roundtrip) also begins at the Chained Rock parking lot. Descend the stairs and turn right (west), hiking along a ridgetop. After crossing an open rock exposure, the path descends more steeply and soon forks; either branch ends at the north side of the **Rock Hotel (RH)**, an impressive recessed cave.

Hikers will note that the route from the Chained Rock lot to the Rock Hotel is all downhill; the return hike, via the same trail, is thus a steady climb (350 feet over 1 mile). Those not fit enough to endure the climb might consider leaving a second car on the Park Road just south of the Rock Hotel; a side trail provides access (see map).

Laurel Cove Trail (LCT). This scenic but moderately strenuous route leads from the Chained Rock Trail to a picnic shelter near the Laurel Cove Amphitheater. The trail is 1.75 miles in length (3.5 miles roundtrip) and is almost all downhill for those starting at the Chained Rock parking lot.

Descend the stairs from the parking lot and turn left (east) on the **Chained Rock Trail (CRT).** After hiking just over .25 mile you will reach a multi-trail intersection, bordered by rock cliffs to the south (see map). Pick up the trail that skirts the east end of these cliffs (the trail was unmarked at the time of our visit) and follow it as it curves to the southwest; this is the **Laurel Cove Trail (LCT).**

The trail soon parallels a forest stream and follows it into a cool, rock-walled ravine. The route through this secluded gorge is negotiated via short stairways and a double switchback. Climbing away from the stream, the trail crosses through a **Natural Arch (NA)** of weathered sandstone and then begins a long, winding descent to the southwest. Near the bottom of the slope, the path enters a cool, moist ravine where rhododendron and eastern hemlock thrive.

The return trip to the Chained Rock lot (via the same route) is almost all uphill; persons not fit enough to endure the climb should leave a second car at the shelter lot (see map) near the Laurel Cove Amphitheater.

The Rock Hotel

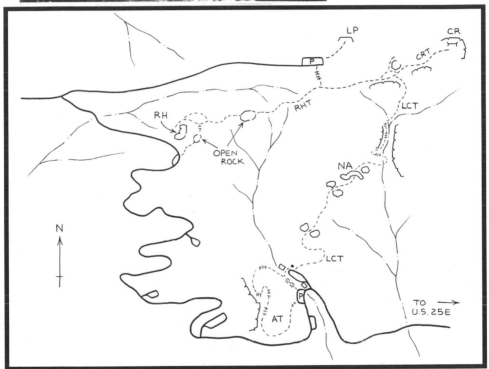

**PINE MOUNTAIN STATE RESORT PARK
(CHAINED ROCK-ROCK HOTEL-LAUREL COVE AREA)**

Azalea Trail (AT). This short (.5 mile) loop begins and ends at a parking lot along the Laurel Cove entry road (see map). Climbing onto a hillside via short stairways and a broad switchback, the trail passes a rampart of sandstone cliffs and then descends to the Laurel Cove Shelter House. Azaleas, not native to this region, were planted along the trail by local garden club members.

62 CUMBERLAND GAP NATIONAL HISTORICAL PARK

Ridge Trail
Distance: 1.8-10.2 miles
roundtrip
Terrain: rolling
Walking time: 1.25-7.0 hours

Sugar Run Trail
Distance: 5.0-11.2 miles
roundtrip
Terrain: hilly
Walking time: 3.0-7.5 hours

Shillalah Creek Trail
Distance: 2.0-6.0 miles
roundtrip
Terrain: hilly
Walking time: 1.5-4.0 hours

Tristate Trail
Distance: 1.5 miles roundtrip
Terrain: hilly
Walking time: 1 hour

Originally thought to be a "wind gap," **Cumberland Gap** is now known to have been carved by a stream which flowed southward from the Middlesboro area to join the Powell River. This stream was later "captured" by Yellow Creek, diverting its flow northward to the Cumberland River. The famous notch, 900 feet deep at its northeastern edge, was traversed by the **Indian Warrior Path** long before it was "discovered" by Dr. Thomas Walker in April of 1750. Daniel Boone and his cohorts crossed through the Gap in 1769 and the **"Wilderness Road"** became the prime route into Kentucky from the south and east.

To preserve the natural beauty of this historic area, **Cumberland Gap National Historical Park** was dedicated on July 4, 1959. Almost 20 miles long and averaging 1.7 miles wide, the Park is draped across **Cumberland Mountain**, from Middlesboro, Kentucky, to Ewing, Virginia; the western end of the Park dips southward into Tennessee. Today, efforts to return the Park to its pre-industrial state are underway: a tunnel through Cumberland Mountain will soon divert U.S. 25E away from the Gap. Access to the Gap and to the remainder of the Park will be maintained by smaller roads and by a network of trails that run atop and along the flanks of Cumberland Mountain.

Directions: From I-75 at Corbin, Kentucky, take Exit 29 and head southeast on U.S. 25E (the Cumberland Gap Parkway). Drive 45.5 miles, passing Pineville and Middlesboro and exit right into the **Visitor Center** area. Maps, exhibits and regional guidebooks, available at the Center, introduce visitors to the topography, geology, history and natural features of the Park.

The road to the **Pinnacle Overlook**, an access point for the **Ridge Trail**, heads east from the Visitor Center and winds up the north flank of Cumberland Mountain.

The trailheads for the **Sugar Run Trail** are along Ky 988. Follow U.S. 25E east from the Visitor Center, drive 1.1 miles and turn left (north) on KY

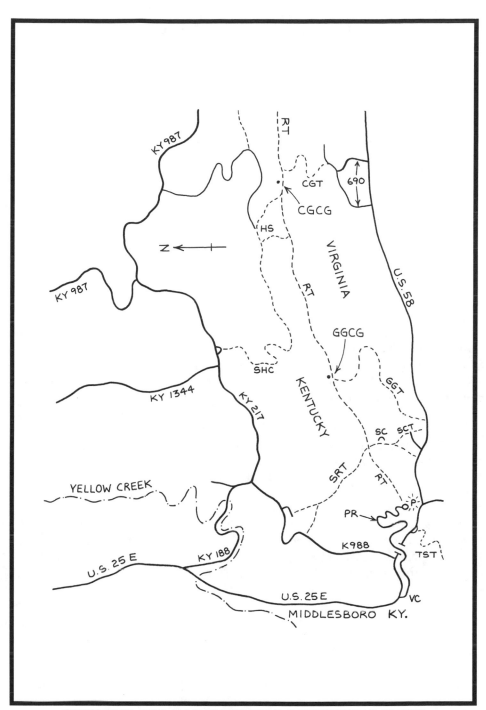

**CUMBERLAND GAP NATIONAL HISTORICAL PARK
(OVERVIEW MAP)**

988. Proceed 1.6 miles to the first trailhead or continue another mile to the Sugar Run Picnic Area.

To reach the **Shillalah Creek Trail**, take Ky 988 north from U.S. 25E as described above. Proceed 3.7 miles and turn right (east) on Ky 217. Drive 5 miles to gravelled pulloffs on both sides of the road; a metal gate crosses the entrance to the **Shillalah Creek Trail** (a wide jeep road), south of Ky 217.

Access to the **Tristate Trail** is off the south side of U.S. 25E, 1.6 miles east of the Visitor Center.

Keep in mind that roadways near the Gap (illustrated on the overview map) will be altered after completion of the U.S. 25E tunnel, which will pass through Cumberland Mountain west of Cumberland Gap.

Routes: Fifty miles of hiking trails provide access to the Park's back-country. We suggest the following day hikes.

Ridge Trail (RT). This 16.6 mile trail follows the crest of Cumberland Mountain from the Pinnacle Overlook to the "White Rocks" north of Ewing, Virginia. In doing so, it follows the border between Kentucky and Virginia as well as the geologic boundary between the Appalachian Plateau, to the northwest, and the Ridge & Valley Province, to the southeast .

The **Ridge Trail** is accessed from the Pinnacle parking lot (see map) or via trails that ascend the flanks of Cumberland Mountain. The **Sugar Run** and **Shillalah Creek Trails** lead up from the Kentucky side while the **Skylight Cave, Gibson Gap, Chadwell Gap** and **Ewing Trails** climb the Virginia wall of Cumberland Mountain; the Virginia Trails are shown on the overview map but were not researched for this guide.

We suggest the following day hikes on the **Ridge Trail**:
> **Pinnacle Overlook (P) to Ridge Trail Shelter (S) - 1.8 miles roundtrip**
> **Pinnacle Overlook (P) to Skylight Cave (SC) - 4.0 miles roundtrip**
> **Pinnacle Overlook (P) to Gibson Gap Campground (GGCG)**
> **- 10.2 miles roundtrip**

Sugar Run Trail (SRT). From the Sugar Run Picnic Area on Ky 988, this trail parallels Sugar Run Creek, gradually climbing through a cool, moist valley adorned with rhododendron and groves of hemlock. Within the first half mile the trail crosses the stream several times and then ascends the valley wall to intersect the other entry path.

The route descends back to the valley floor where it crosses a tributary and then follows Sugar Run Creek to the crest of Cumberland Mountain. Nearing the top of the ridge, the trail splits away from the main creek and soon intersects the **Ridge** and **Skylight Cave Trails.**

We suggest the following day hikes via the **Sugar Run Trail**:
> **Sugar Run Picnic Area to Skylight Cave (SC) - 5 miles roundtrip**
> **Sugar Run Picnic Area to Pinnacle Overlook (P) - 8 miles roundtrip**
> **Sugar Run Picnic Area to Gibson Gap Campground (GGCG)**
> **- 11.2 miles roundtrip**

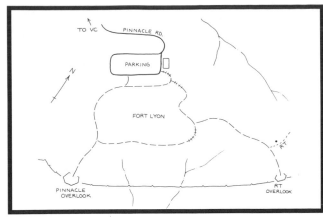

**PINNACLE
OVERLOOK
AREA**

*Looking west from
the Pinnacle*

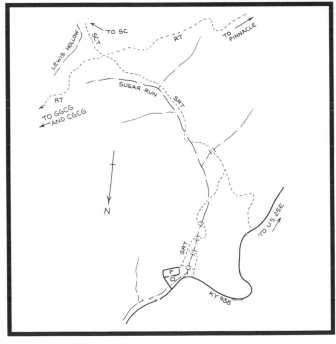

**SUGAR RUN
TRAIL**

Shillalah Creek Trail (SHC). This wide, graveled jeep road leaves the south side of Ky 217 and climbs southwestward at a moderate grade. Watch for wild turkeys which often forage along the road. Nearing Shillalah Creek, the route angles to the SSE, passing scenic rock formations and several waterfalls; a side path leads out to one of these cascades (see map).

Two long switchbacks take you higher along the south flank of Brush Mountain. During the colder months, views extend across the Shillalah Creek Valley to Cumberland Mountain. The trail continues eastward to the **Hensley Settlement (HS)** and the **Chadwell Gap Campground (CGCG)** but these destinations are a bit long for day hikes.

We suggest the following day hikes via the **Shillalah Creek Trail**:
> **Shillalah Creek Trailhead to Waterfalls - 2.0 miles roundtrip**
> **Shillalah Creek Trailhead to crest of Brush Mountain (where a second path from Ky 217 intersects the trail) - 6.0 miles roundtrip**

Tristate Trail (TST). This .75 mile trail (1.5 miles roundtrip) leads from a parking area on U.S. 25E to a hilltop marker where the State lines of Kentucky, Tennessee and Virginia converge. From the parking lot the trail climbs southward via a series of switchbacks, using a section of the old Wilderness Road along the way. After passing the former site of a Union Commissary (C), the trail leaves the Wilderness Road near the old entrance to Fort Foote and angles to the east, climbing more steeply.

Another .25 mile brings you to the **Tristate Pavilion** and a **National Historic Civil Engineering Landmark.** After a picnic lunch at the "Tristate Junction," return to your car via the same route.

The Tristate Pavilion

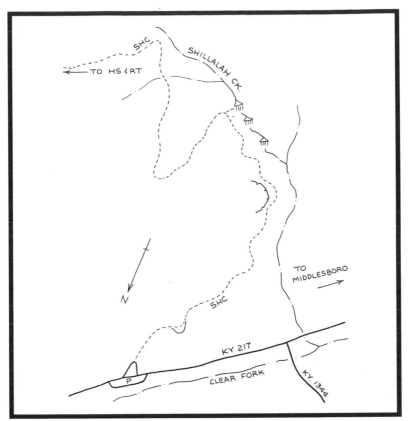

SHILLALAH CREEK TRAIL

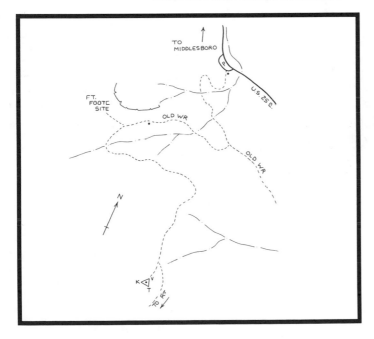

**TRISTATE
TRAIL**

IX. SPECIAL HIKING AREAS

Most of the Hiking Areas in this guide are free and open to the public throughout the year. A few, such as Columbus-Belmont State Park and Sloughs Wildlife Management Area, are open on a seasonal basis and Bernheim Arboretum & Forest, operated by a nonprofit foundation, charges an environmental impact fee on weekends and holidays.

This chapter introduces the reader to other hiking areas in Kentucky that are accessible by special arrangement only. Specific directions are not given in order to protect these sensitive preserves.

Lilley Cornett Woods. Designated a National Natural Landmark and managed by Eastern Kentucky University, this 554 acre ecological research station protects a 252 acre remnant of virgin, mixed-mesophytic forest. Ninety species of trees and shrubs are found within this Letcher County preserve, which harbors a few giants that are more than 350 years old.

Open daily from May 15 through August 15 and weekends, April through October, the refuge can be toured by taking either a 2 or 4 hour, guided hike. For more information, call 606-633-5828.

Blackacre State Nature Preserve. Used as an environmental education center by Jefferson County Schools and the University of Louisville, this 170 acre refuge, near Jeffersontown, features a 19th Century working farm. Emphasis is placed on the potential harmony of nature and agriculture. For information on guided tours of the preserve, contact the Kentucky State Nature Preserve Commission at 502-573-2886.

Vernon Douglas State Nature Preserve. Located in Hardin County, this 730 acre preserve was dedicated in August, 1992. The refuge protects one of the most mature second-growth forests within Kentucky's "Knob Belt." A trail system runs through Hall Hollow and atop adjacent ridges. Parking is currently limited to roadsides but improved access is planned in the near future. For more information, contact the Kentucky State Nature Preserve Commission at 502-573-2886.

Six Mile Island State Nature Preserve. Dedicated in June, 1979, this 81 acre island is located in the Ohio River, near Louisville. Protection was established in order to allow this unique riverine island to return to its natural state. Access is by boat only and there are no facilities or developed trails at this time. For more information, contact the Kentucky State Nature Preserve Commission at 502-573-2886.

Dinsmore Woods State Nature Preserve. This 106 acre preserve, near Burlington, in Boone County, protects a mature maple-oak-ash forest. Trails have been developed but access is by special permission only. Contact the Kentucky State Nature Preserve Commission at 502-573-2886.

Massacre Trail. Open twice each year, on the first Saturday in April and the first Saturday in November, this 12 mile route, in Middletown, Kentucky, honors the pioneer men and women who carved Jefferson County from the Kentucky wilderness. The trail is named for two massacres that occured along its route: the murder of Abraham Lincoln (the President's grandfather) in May, 1786, and the assault on the Richard Chenoweth family by Shawnee Indians, in July, 1789.

The trail begins at the Middletown Christian Church, at 11508 Main St.; using a network of secondary roads, the route crosses rolling terrain and can be covered by most individuals within 7-8 hours. Pre-registration is not required and Scouts can earn a Hiking Merit Badge by completing an extended, 20 mile route. For more information, write to Historic Middletown, Inc., Box 43013, Middletown, Kentucky 40253-0013.

APPENDIX I.
THE NATURAL HISTORY OF KENTUCKY

A knowledge of Kentucky's natural history will add to your enjoyment of the hikes in this guide. More importantly, we hope that it increases your commitment to protecting what remains of the State's natural heritage.

Precambrian Era (4600-600 MYA*)

Precambrian time, the earth's first 4 billion years, was characterized by violent earthquakes, relentless volcanic activity, gradual cooling of the planet's crust, formation of the atmosphere and evolution of the primordial seas. The ancient Precambrian rocks (igneous and metamorphic in character) are the foundation of the continental plates. Paleozoic, Mesozoic and Cenozoic deposits have since accumulated on this basement rock. Precambrian rock is exposed where it has been thrust upward to form mountain ranges (e.g. the Rocky Mountains), where glaciers have scoured away the overlying sediments (e.g. the Canadian Shield) or where rivers have cut deep into the earth's crust (e.g. the Grand Canyon).

Life evolved in Precambrian seas some 3.6 billion years ago, protected from intense solar radiation by the ocean waters. Among the earliest life forms were cyanobacteria and primitive algae which, by the process of photosynthesis, gradually enriched the earth's atmosphere with oxygen.

Paleozoic Era (600-225 MYA)

By the onset of the Paleozoic Era, a tremendous diversity of marine invertebrates had evolved. Brachiopods, bryozoans and trilobites reached their zenith during the **Cambrian (600-500 MYA)** and **Ordovician (500-440 MYA) Periods**. Shallow seas bathed much of North America during the Paleozoic Era, depositing limestones, shales and sandstones across the continent. Ordovician limestones and shales, rich with the fossils of early marine life, are exposed throughout the Bluegrass Region of Kentucky; an upward bowing of the deeper, Precambrian rock, known as the "Cincinnati Arch," has brought these ancient sea deposits near the surface. Examine any roadcut or stream bed in northern Kentucky and you will find these sedimentary rocks.

During the **Silurian Period (440-400 MYA)**, the atmospheric ozone layer had thickened sufficiently to allow the first land plants to colonize coastal areas. Throughout the remainder of the Paleozoic Era, these pioneer plants would evolve into a tremendous diversity of ferns, horsetails and primitive conifers. It was during the **Carboniferous Period (350-270 MYA)** that extensive swamplands covered much of the globe; home to giant amphibians and the first reptiles, these carbon-rich wetlands would later decompose to produce the thick coal seams of the Appalachian Plateau.

*MYA - million years ago

The Carboniferous Period is subdivided into the **Mississippian (350-310 MYA)** and the **Pennsylvanian (310-270 MYA) Periods.** Mississippian limestones, deposited in shallow seas, are especially well developed across central and southern Kentucky. Subject to dissolution by ground water and protected by an overlying cap of sandstone, these limestone formations harbor numerous cave systems, including the world's most extensive network of caverns, **Mammoth Cave**.

Pennsylvanian sandstones, deposited along seashores and river banks, cover much of eastern Kentucky. As the North American and African plates collided, late in the Paleozoic Era, folding, faulting and uplift occured along what is now the Appalachian Mountain Chain. A broad area west of this Range was also uplifted, giving rise to the Appalachian Plateau, a geologic province that stretches from east-central New York to northern Alabama. Unlike the folding and faulting that occured in the mountain range, the Plateau strata were left intact, a virtual layer-cake of sedimetary rock. Capped by resistant, Pennsylvanian sandstone, the Appalachian Plateau has since been carved into a maze of valleys and ridges by a vast network of streams.

This natural arch at Pine Mountain State Resort Park
is composed of Carboniferous sandstone

Mesozoic Era (225-65 MYA)

The land that is now Kentucky either remained above the level of Mesozoic seas or their sediments have since eroded from the surface; an exception is in extreme southwestern Kentucky where Cretaceous sea deposits are exposed along the Tennessee and Cumberland Rivers.

The Mesozoic Era is divided into three periods: the **Triassic**, the **Jurassic** and the **Cretaceous Periods**. By the onset of the **Triassic Period (225-190 MYA)**, the earth's land masses had congregated into the "super continent" of Pangea. A hot, dry climate set the stage for the "Age of Reptiles." Turtles, primitive crocodiles and small, herbivorous dinosaurs appeared during the Triassic Period.

The **Jurassic Period (190-135 MYA)** witnessed the evolution of large dinosaurs (allosaurus, brontosaurus, stegosaurus), the appearance of flowering plants, the debut of primitive birds and the inglorious arrival of small, shrew-like creatures...the first mammals. Pangea split into Laurasia, the northern continents, and Gondwanaland, the southern continents, during the Jurassic. Primitive monotremes and marsupials evolved on Gondwanaland while the first eutherians (placental mammals) spread across Laurasia. Tyrannosaurus rex and the horned dinosaurs ruled the **Cretaceous Period (135-65)** during which a broad seaway covered much of central North America.

Cenozoic Era (65 MYA-Present)

Cooling of the earth's climate, whether due to continental shifts, increased volcanic activity or to the impact of a devastating meteor, set the stage for the demise of the dinosaurs and the rise of mammalian life. The Rocky Mountains pushed skyward as the Cenozoic Era dawned, producing a vast "rain shadow" across central North America. Semi-arid conditions in this region favored the evolution of prairie grasslands; in turn, these nutritious plains enticed small, reclusive mammals from the surrounding forests, leading to the evolution of the "mega-fauna" that characterized the mid Cenozoic. Primitive camels, rhinoceros and horses appeared in North America, later spreading to Asia via the Bering land bridge. Conversely, ancestral bison, mammoths and mastodons, having evolved in Asia, spread eastward to North America.

Such inter-continental migrations occured during periods of glaciation when sea levels fell and "land bridges" opened between the continents. Glacial activity reached its peak during the **Pleistocene Epoch (2-.01 MYA)**, commonly known as the "Ice Age." Forming in Canada, glaciers advanced into the continental U.S. at least four times during the Pleistocene, retreating northward during relatively warm, "inter-glacial periods." While none of these Ice Sheets entered Kentucky, their effects are nevertheless apparent in the Bluegrass State. The **Kansan Glacier**, which pushed southward some 1.2 million years ago, blocked the course of the Teays River, a giant waterway that headed in the Virginia Appalachians and flowed northwestward to the upper Mississippi Valley. The waters of the Teays River were thus diverted southward, triggering the evolution of the Ohio River System; the Ohio's course was later molded by the **Illinoian Glacier** (400,000 years ago), the southernmost glacial advance during the Pleistocene. Outwash from the Kansan Glacier compacted into conglomerate rock which is now exposed along the mid Ohio Valley (see Boone County Cliffs State Nature Preserve, Hiking Area #33).

A cool, moist "peri-glacial" zone spread just south of the Pleistocene glaciers, favoring the development of extensive coniferous forests. As the last Ice Sheet (the **Wisconsin Glacier**) retreated into Canada, these forests advanced northward and were slowly replaced by the mixed-mesophytic hardwoods that dominate the landscape today. Pockets of hemlock, remnants from the Pleistocene, still thrive in the cool, shaded valleys of the Appalachian Plateau.

Torrents of meltwater carved and widened the Ohio, Missouri and Mississippi Valleys and deposited layers of sand and gravel across the lowlands that border these Rivers. Such loose, Quaternary sediments underlie the sandy soil of westernmost Kentucky. Freed from the weight of the ice, the Midwest Region literally rebounded upward, further augmenting flow through the central river system. Tallgrass prairie, fed by the glacial till, spread across the upper Mississippi watershed.

Man evolved in East Africa during the latter half of the Pleistocene; by the end of the Epoch, his influence was felt across all continents except Antarctica. Paleohunters crossed the Bering land bridge during the Wisconsin Glaciation and were likely south of the Ice Sheet by 15-20,000 years ago. Following herds of mammoth and bison, these nomads were the first human Americans. By the onset of the **Holocene Period (.01 MYA to the Present)**, prehistoric North Americans had adopted an "archaic" lifestyle, with relatively permanent settlements.

"Modern" Indian tribes occupied Kentucky by the 1600s. The Shawnee controlled the Ohio Valley while the domain of the Cherokee stretched from southeastern Kentucky to the Great Smokey Mountains. These Native Americans enjoyed an unspoiled wilderness, teeming with life. Spring and fall migrations brought huge flocks of geese, ducks and other waterfowl to the lakes, marshes and rivers of the Ohio and Mississippi Valleys. Deer, bison and wild turkey were plentiful throughout the region and both black bear and cougar roamed the forested hills of the Appalachian Plateau. Bald eagles searched for trout along the crystal clear streams and passenger pigeons, now extinct, darkened the sky with their massive flights.

The first white settlers reached Kentucky territory during the late 1700s. Daniel Boone and his cohorts crossed through the Cumberland Gap in 1769 while other pioneers floated westward on the Ohio River, establishing settlements along its banks. "Losantiville," present-day Cincinnati was founded in 1788 and Newport, Kentucky, was platted seven years later. The rest is history!

APPENDIX II.
KENTUCKY CONSERVATION ORGANIZATIONS

As you hike the forests, meadows and marshlands of Kentucky, keep in mind that these natural areas are under constant threat from human activity: pollution, "resource recovery," suburban sprawl and other forms of "development" all take their toll. The State's native flora and fauna, especially the endangered species, are threatened more by habitat loss than by any other natural or man-induced phenomenon. You can help to preserve and protect Kentucky's wild lands by donating time and/or money to the organizations listed below. This is but a partial list of the groups that are working to protect what remains of the State's natural heritage.

Abraham Lincoln Birthplace National Historic Site, National Park Service, U.S. Dept. of the Interior, 2995 Lincoln Farm Rd., Hodgenville, KY 42748; 502-358-3137

Berea College Forest, CPO 605, Berea, KY 40404; 606-986-9341, Ext. 5587

Big South Fork National River & Recreation Area, Superintendent's Office, Route 3, Box 401, Oneida, TN 37841

Cumberland Gap National Historical Park, National Park Service, Dept. of the Interior, Box 1848, Middlesboro, KY 40965; 606-248-2817

Daniel Boone National Forest, Forest Supervisor, 100 Vaught Rd., Winchester, KY 40391, 606-745-3100
    Berea Ranger District, 1835 Big Hill Road, Berea, KY 40403 606-986-8434
    London Ranger District, Box 907, U.S. Highway 25 South, London, KY 40743; 606-864-4163
    Morehead Ranger District, 2375 Kentucky 801 South, Morehead, KY 40351; 606-784-5624
    Redbird Ranger District, HC 68, Box 65, Big Creek, KY 40914; 606-598-2192
    Somerset Ranger District, 156 Realty Lane, Somerset, KY 42501; 606-679-2018
    Stanton Ranger District, 705 W. College Ave., Stanton, KY 40380; 606-663-2852
    Stearns Ranger District, U.S. Highway 27 North, Box 429, Whitley City, KY 42653; 606-376-5323

Eastern Kentucky University, Division of Natural Areas, Richmond, KY 40475; 606-622-1476

Friends of Bernheim, Isaac W. Bernheim Foundation, Clermont, KY 40110
502-955-8512

Greenspace, Inc., City Hall, Elizabethtown, KY 42701

Historic Middletown, Inc., Box 43013, Middletown, KY 40253-0013

Jefferson County Memorial Forest, Box 467, 12304 Holsclaw Hill Road,
Fairdale, KY 40118; 502-366-5432

Jenny Wiley Trail Volunteer Program, c/o State Naturalist, Kentucky
Department of Parks, Capitol Plaza Tower, Frankfort, KY 40601
502-564-5410

Kentucky Department of Fish & Wildlife Resources, #1 Game Farm Rd.,
Frankfort, KY 40601

**Kentucky Department of Natural Resources and Environmental Protec-
tion**, Frankfort, KY 40601; 502-564-6716

Kentucky State Forests
Tygarts & Olympia State Forests, District Forester, 749 W. First,
Morehead, KY 40351; 606-784-7504
Pennyrile State Forest, District Forester, Box 465, Madisonville,
KY 42431; 502-825-6527
Kentucky Ridge & Kentenia State Forests, District Forester, Box
130, Pineville, KY 40977; 606-337-3011

Kentucky State Nature Preserve Commission, 801 Schenkel Lane, Frankfort, KY 40601; 502-573-2886

Kentucky State Parks, 500 Mero St., 11th Floor, Capitol Plaza Tower,
Frankfort, KY 40601; 502-564-2172

Land Between the Lakes, 100 Van Morgan Dr., Golden Pond, KY 42211-9001
502-924-5602

Lexington-Fayette Urban County Division of Parks & Recreation, 545 N.
Upper St., Lexington, KY 40508; 606-288-2900

Lilley Cornett Woods, Skyline, KY 41851; 606-633-5828

Mammoth Cave National Park, National Park Service, Mammoth Cave,
KY 42259; 502-758-2251

Metro Parks of Louisville, Box 37280, Louisville, KY 40233-7080

National Audubon Society, Clyde E. Buckley Wildlife Sanctuary, 1305 Germany Rd., Frankfort, KY 40601-9240; 606-873-5711

National Audubon Society, Great Lakes Regional Office, 692 North High Street, Suite 208, Columbus, Ohio 43215-1548; 614-224-3303

The Nature Conservancy, Kentucky Field Office, 642 W. Main St., Lexington, KY 40508; 606-259-9655

Sierra Club, Cumberland Chapter, 259 West Short St., Lexington, KY 40507

BIBLIOGRAPHY

Clark, Regina V., Dick Patterson and Scott Seiber, **A Guide to Land Between the Lakes**, 1992

Coleman, Brenda D. and JoAnna Smith, **Hiking the Big South Fork**, University of Tennessee Press, Knoxville, 1989 (Second Edition, 1993)

Daniel Boone National Forest, Recreation Guide R8-RG40, Forest Service Southern Region, U. S. Department of Agriculture, Revised 5/93

The Daniel Boone National Forest, Kentucky, U. S. Forest Service, Department of Agriculture, General Report to the Public for 1992

Edwards, Stephen M., **The Origin of Highland Cemetery**, July, 1986

Farb, Peter, **Face of North America, The Natural History of a Continent**, Harper & Row, 1963

Folzenlogen, Darcy and Robert, **Walking Cincinnati, Scenic Hikes Through the Parks & Neighborhoods of Greater Cincinnati and Northern Kentucky**, Second Edition, Willow Press, 1993

A Guide to Public Wildlife Areas in Kentucky, Kentucky Department of Fish & Wildlife Resources, March, 1989

Henson, Ed, Editor, **Kentucky Trails**, Director of Recreation, Kentucky Department of Parks, Commonwealth of Kentucky

Hiking, Daniel Boone National Forest, Stearns Ranger District, Forest Service South Region, U. S. Department of Agriculture

Hiking Guide to the Sheltowee Trace National Recreation Trail, London Ranger District, Daniel Boone National Forest, U. S. Forest Service, Department of Agriculture

Jenny Wiley Trail, Carsonite, JWT-1285, 1989

Kentucky Outdoors, Kentucky Department of Travel Development in cooperation with Kentucky Standard Special Publications, 1993

Luckett, William W., **Cumberland Gap National Historical Park**, Reprinted from Tennessee Historical Quarterly, Vol. XXIII, December, 1964, No. 4

McFarlan, Arthur C., **Geology of Kentucky**, University of Kentucky, 1943

Moize, Elizabeth A. with photography by William Strode, **"Daniel Boone, First Hero of the Frontier,"** National Geographic, Vol. 168, No. 6, December, 1985

Ruchhoft, Robert H., **Kentucky's Land of the Arches**, Pucelle Press, 1986

Sides, Stanley D., **Guide to the Surface Trails of Mammoth Cave National Park**, Cave Books, St. Louis, Missouri, 1991

Stearn, C.S.. R.L. Carrol and T.H. Clark, **Geological Evolution of North America**, 3rd Edition, John Wiley & Sons, Inc., 1979

Sullivan, Jerry and Glenda Daniels, **Hiking Trails in the Southern Mountains**, Contemporary Books Inc., Chicago, 1975

Thornbury, William D., **Regional Geomorphology of the United States**, John Wiley & Sons, Inc., 1965

Weis, Deborah A., editor, **Kentucky, A Traveler's Guide, The Uncommonwealth of Kentucky**, Kentucky Department of Travel Development, January, 1991

Wengert, Richard H., **Recreation on the Daniel Boone Trail**, Forest Supervisor, Daniel Boone National Forest

INDEX

NOTES

NOTES

NOTES

NOTES

NOTES

NOTES